Finance for Non-Financial Managers

TABLE OF CONTENTS

DISCLAIMER

THE IMPORTANCE OF ACCURATE FINANCIAL DATA

ANALYSIS

Financial statements in modern business are an important source of information for decision making. Realistic and objective accounting is one of the necessary preconditions for business decision-making. The purpose of general financial statements is to provide information about the financial position, financial performance, and cash flows of a business entity that is useful to a wide range of users in making economic decisions.

The financial report is the most complete system of communication and interpretation of business and financial activities. It is also relevant to the financial reporting system and the analysis of financial statements. The financial report is a true and fair statement of financial operations and activities of the company because in the process of its preparation the following is respected:

1. The principle of accounting prudence (not over or underestimating values) to avoid the risk of uncertainty

2. The cost principle (historical cost) for valuing balance sheet items, unless otherwise determined

3. Principle of obligatory consent, i.e. adherence to rules and procedures

4. Inter-periodic consistency of application of established principles

5. Conscientious application of accounting principles

When preparing financial statements, in the context of the quality of financial statements, it is necessary to pay attention to the rules of preparation and presentation of financial statements. Financial statements are the responsibility of the company's leadership because leadership is the only one authorized to use the company's resources. The financial statements provide a picture of the effectiveness of the use of these resources. Furthermore, financial statements are prepared by accounting and employees in accounting, so they are not relieved of responsibility.

The financial report is essentially a carrier of information. For information to be useful, it should contain a message that is true and complete (syntactic aspect), written in an appropriate terminology that is clear and understandable to users (semantic aspect), strive to meet user needs, and reduce uncertainty (pragmatic aspect).

The importance of financial analysis itself is seen primarily from the aspect of management and development of the company itself. A good financial plan must take into account the good qualities of the company and its weaknesses. The crucial task of analyzing financial statements is to identify the good qualities of the company and the financial manager must plan their financial conditions.

In general, there are three main objectives of the financial statements:

1. Providing financial information to users

Financial statements are reports that are prepared based on the financial activities of an enterprise. Activity data is managed and provides information on the financial position, asset status, business results, etc.

Such information can be used by users as a reference in decision making. In this case, the user can mean the owner, shareholders, creditors, etc.

2. Management accountability tool

In addition to providing information, financial statements are used as a management accountability tool. Management reports on what has been done in one period. And the report can be a reference to whether the financial activities were performed properly or not.

Therefore, there can be no value errors in financial statements. Each number that appears must have proof, for example, backed by proof of the transaction. Financial statements can also be used to detect whether there are irregularities in the use of company finances.

3. Material evaluation

In addition to the existence of financial statements, companies provide detailed information on the financial flow and its use. This report can be a reference for determining a company's success by assessing whether the goals for one period have been met or not.

Furthermore, the report can assess the company's assessment of the strengths and weaknesses of activities carried out in one period. Companies can cut costs that are considered less efficient and allocate finances to more cost-effective activities.

Bad interpretation of financial statements may arise in connection with the recognition, measurement, presentation, or disclosure of elements of the financial statements. Reasons for errors should be sought in the absence of information, misjudgment of a particular business event or financial performance of a transaction, ignorance, or ultimately, intent to misrepresent, which implies fraudulent financial reporting.

Poor accounting and finance can result in the non-acquisition of loans, subsequently assessed taxes, mistrust of business partners due to poor business decisions, and in the long run even loss of assets or business. After all, the management of a company is responsible for the accuracy of its financial statements. Therefore, the quality and professional competencies of the employees in the accounting service should be a criterion that weighs the price of the service.

Especially in times of crisis, cooperation between accounting services and management is very important. Maybe the last business year was worse than the previous one, so it is even more important how the company presented the basic information: the relationship between customers and suppliers, the amount of financial liabilities, the ratio of financial liabilities to the maturity of assets; capital to finance operations, turnover of funds and so on. Too often, banks give companies a worse credit rating and then a lower borrowing limit as a consequence of poor accounting presentation. This can mean fewer loans at a higher interest rate. In the worst case, the credit rating committee even rejects the company.

A good accounting service cooperates with the company. An entrepreneur can turn to them for advice even when embarking on new business challenges. The vast majority of entrepreneurs make their further business decisions on accounting analyzes. In this sense, trust must be high. One of the views on how to determine a good accounting service is also that the service needs to be big enough to offer the customer trust, but at the same time, it needs to work in a sense to offer the customer exactly what the customer wants. The quality of services comes first, followed by knowledge of the law, training and advice, and information on developments. Companies need the accounting service to provide them with relevant information during operation, as those are the kind of information needed for making appropriate business decisions. In this way, the company will avoid exceeding the legally allowed limits, and quality accounting service will of course record all the business events accurately, the financial statements will be correct in content, and there will be no unnecessary unrecognized costs in tax returns and possible inspection procedures. And secondly, the right balance sheets will enable the company to perform sovereignly at the bank, in public tenders, in front of business partners, and in front of other users of the business information.

THE INCOME STATEMENT

The preparation of profit and loss accounts (income statement) depends on the provisions of existing accounting regulations. The income statement may be prescribed by law or proposed by a professional organization.

The income statement can be presented in the form of a one-sided or two-sided account, however, due to the greater expressive power, a one-sided account is most often used. It enables the segmentation of income and expenses, i.e. the presentation of results according to the types of activities.

If the income statement is in the form of a two-sided account, expenses with a positive financial result are shown on the left, and income and a negative financial result are shown on the right. If the income statement is in the form of a one-sided account, first the income is stated, then the expenses, and finally the financial result as the difference between them.

The income statement provides information on how much income, expenses, profit, loss was generated, and how much income tax liability arose from the company's operations in a certain period.

The income statement is a financial report that shows the performance and business activity of a company over a period of time. It contains a presentation of all income and expenses, and the achieved financial result in a certain accounting period. It gives us the answer to the question of whether the company has achieved its financial goal – profitability.

Revenue is the value of goods and services sold that are reported during the accounting period. An increase in revenue affects the capital increase. In addition to income from regular activities, other types of income may occur, such as income from interest, exchange rate differences, surpluses on stock, use of goods for own needs, etc.

Expenses are costs contained in products and services sold. These include employee salaries, rents, service costs, depreciation, interest, etc. They are also often referred to as operating costs and lead to a reduction in capital.

Below are presented income statements of a manufacturing company for two consecutive years.

	Amount in thousands		Structure		Index
	Current year	Previous year	Current year	Previous year	
TOTAL INCOME (I + V + VII)	815,087	882,711	100.00%	100.00%	92.3391
TOTAL EXPENSE (II + VI + VIII)	656,023	671,931	80.49%	76.12%	97.6325
A. OPERATING INCOME AND EXPENSES					
I. OPERATING INCOME (1 + 2 + 3-4 + 5)	807,044	869,303	99.01%	98.48%	92.8381
1. Sales revenue	791,482	856,578	97.10%	97.04%	92.4005
2. Revenues from activation of effects and goods			0.00%	0.00%	0
3. Increasing the value of performance stocks	14,782	12,593	1.81%	1.43%	117.383
4. Decrease in the value of performance stocks			0.00%	0.00%	0
5. Other operating income	780	132	0.10%	0.01%	590.909
II. OPERATING EXPENSES (1 to 5)	640,466	670,367	78.58%	75.94%	95.5396
1. Cost of goods sold			0.00%	0.00%	0
2. Material costs	581,767	621,610	71.37%	70.42%	93.5904
3. Wage costs, wage compensation and other personal expenses	8,575	9,496	1.05%	1.08%	90.3012

4. Depreciation and provisions costs	11,832	9,567	1.45%	1.08%	123.675
5. Other operating expenses	38,292	29,694	4.70%	3.36%	128.955
III. OPERATING PROFIT (I-II)	166,578	198,936	20.44%	22.54%	83.7345
IV. OPERATING LOSS (II-I)	0	0	0.00%	0.00%	0
V. FINANCIAL INCOME	6,845	12,441	0.84%	1.41%	55.0197
VI. FINANCIAL EXPENSES	6,556	574	0.80%	0.07%	1142.16
VII. OTHER INCOME	1,198	967	0.15%	0.11%	123.888
VIII. OTHER EXPENSES	9,001	990	1.10%	0.11%	909.192
IX. OPERATING PROFIT (III-IV + V-VI + VII-VIII)	159,064	210,780	19.51%	23.88%	75.4645
X. LOSS FROM REGULAR OPERATIONS (IV-III-IV + V-VIII + VII)	0	0	0.00%	0.00%	0
XI. NET PROFIT FROM DISCONTINUED OPERATIONS			0.00%	0.00%	0
XII. NET LOSS FROM DISCONTINUED OPERATIONS	8	3	0.00%	0.00%	266.667
B. PROFIT BEFORE TAX (IX + XI-X-XII)	159,056	210,777	19.51%	23.88%	75.4617
C. LOSS BEFORE TAX (X + XII-IX-XI)	0	0	0.00%	0.00%	0
D. INCOME TAX			0.00%	0.00%	0
1. Tax expense period	25,422	16,571	3.12%	1.88%	153.413
2. Deferred tax expenses period		84	0.00%	0.01%	0
3. Deferred tax income period	204	0	0.03%	0.00%	0

14

E. Paid personal income to the employer			0.00%	0.00%	0
F. NET PROFIT (B-C-1-2 + 3-E)	133,838	194,122	16.42%	21.99%	68.9453
G. NET LOSS (C-B + 1 + 2-3 + E)	0	0	0.00%	0.00%	0
H. NET PROFIT BELONGING TO MINORITY INVESTORS			0.00%	0.00%	0
I. NET PROFIT BELONGING TO OWNERS OF THE PARENT LEGAL ENTITY			0.00%	0.00%	0
J. EARNINGS PER SHARE			0.00%	0.00%	0
1. Basic earnings per share			0.00%	0.00%	0
2. Earnings per share reductions			0.00%	0.00%	0

The main goal of the Income Statement is to calculate the achieved periodic operating result. Determining the incurred expenses and income in the previous accounting period creates the conditions for calculating their difference, which is manifested as a positive or negative financial result (profit or loss). In modern business conditions, it is inevitable to determine the achieved business result for a certain accounting period. Thus, leadership and management want to see the effects of the efforts undertaken in the business of the company to consider the effectiveness of the applied solutions for the realization of this goal.

For the successful operation of the company in the long run, in addition to taking into account the financial situation, the company must operate with a positive result, ie that the company's revenues exceed the expenses that preceded them during the business. Therefore, the main goal of the Income Statement is to measure or determine business results for economic control of operations and disposal of company funds

From what we can see above, in the Income Statement Structure, operating revenues account for 99.01% of total revenues in the current year or 98.48% in the previous year (Line I). The high % share of operating revenues is understandable since operating revenues arise as a result of the basic activity of the company. The growth of operating revenues in the current year can be attributed to the decrease in financial revenues in the current year.

In the structure of business income, it is important that sales revenue dominates, which actually converts stocks of products, goods, and services into cash needed for the continuous continuation of the company's business process. This is exactly the situation in the observed company. Within operating revenues, sales revenues play a dominant role, amounting to 97.10% in the current year and 97.04% in the previous year (Line I.1). The share of other operating income in total operating income is less than 0.1% in both years and is not significant.

Dynamically, there is a tendency to reduce financial income from 1.41% in the previous to 0.84% in the current year (Line V).

The share of total income on operating expenses in the structure of the income statement shows a tendency of growth in the current year compared to the previous year by 2.64% and so in the current year it amounts to 78.58% (Line II). The largest share in the structure of operating expenses is realized by material costs from 71.37% in the current year to 70.42% in the previous year (Line II.2).

The reduction of operating income with gross salaries is conditioned by the increase in salaries. Gross salaries burden the operating income of the observed company with 1.05% in the current year, or 1.08% in the previous year. On the other hand, depreciation and provisioning costs burden the operating income of the observed company with 11.8% of the current year, and 9.57% of the previous year.

Dynamically, there were no significant changes in either gross wages or depreciation and provisions costs compared to the previous year.

The share of operating profit in operating income shows which part (what percentage) of operating income falls on operating profit. In our example, in the observed company, it amounts to 20.44% in the current year and 22.54% in the previous year.

Also, in absolute terms, profit from ordinary activities accounts for 19.51% of total revenues in the current year and 23.88% in the previous year (Line IX). As we can see, there is a decrease. Most of it can be attributed to the decline in the sales revenues, and of course, the increase in the expenses. However, the analysis of the income statement shows that this company is successful in its business. A positive financial result in both years, stable liquidity, and acceptable indebtedness are just some of the indicators that speak in favor of this.

BALANCE SHEET ANALYSIS

A balance sheet is a systematic review of assets, liabilities, and equity at a particular date, i.e. at the balance sheet date. It is also a complete statistical financial report that provides information on the financial position or condition of the company. It serves as a basis for assessing business security. There are two aspects of a company's financial position that financial managers must examine, and these are:

- The current or short-term financial position of the business entity or liquidity

- The long-term financial position of the business entity or solvency.

Long-term financial position can be jeopardized by a weak current financial position and vice versa. However, the long-term financial position is far less affected by the change to the short-term, one example being seasonal fluctuations.

The balance sheet consists of the assets of the business entity, and the source of assets liabilities, which represent the principal and liabilities of the business entity.

The balance sheet provides answers to questions such as:

- What is the financial power of the company?

- What is the liquidity?

- What is the indebtedness?

- What is the ratio of own and other people's financing of the property, i.e. what is the horizontal financial structure?

- What is the position of the company compared to the previous period?

- What is the position of the observed company compared to companies of similar activity?

The answers to the above provide the basis for judging the financial position of the observed entity, for identifying weaknesses and shortcomings in business, but also for predicting the future. There are so many risks that need to be identified and addressed on time, such as the high availability of funds that may suggest an impending financial crisis, which can easily transform into an economic crisis, so borrowing should be especially prudent. The balance sheet provides answers to such questions.

The structure of the balance sheet depends on the criteria for classifying balance sheet items. The following criteria are known:

- liquidity (decreasing and increasing)

- security

- maturity

ASSETS	LIABILITIES
• RECEIVABLES FOR SUBSCRIBED BUT UNPAID CAPITAL • FIXED ASSETS • CURRENT ASSETS • PAID EXPENSES FOR THE FUTURE PERIOD AND ACCRUED INCOME • LOSS OVER CAPITAL	• CAPITAL AND RESERVES • RESERVATIONS • LONG TERM LIABILITIES • SHORT - TERM LIABILITIES • DEFERRED PAYMENT OF EXPENSES AND ACCRUED INCOME AND FUTURE INCOME
TOTAL ASSETS	TOTAL LIABILITIES
Off-balance sheet	Off-balance sheet

Balance Sheet Structure

The goal of the balance sheet analysis is to assess the financial position and profitability. Profitability is an increase in equity based on the financial result. However, the financial result itself is complex because it comes from operating, financial, and non-business income. If two companies in the absolute amount have the same financial result and at the same time differ in the amounts from which the financial result originates, then it is a different quality. On the other hand, the risk of achieving a financial result may be higher or lower, which is also important for assessing profitability. Finally, a company may have a poor financial position and a negative financial result. In such circumstances, the balance sheet analysis must answer whether or not the company can improve its financial position (bring it back to normal) and whether or not the company can get out of the loss zone. Accordingly, the objectives of the balance sheet analysis are:

- Structure and dynamics of total income and distribution of total income, source of financial result, risk of achieving a financial result, profitability, and possibility to get out of the loss zone.

- Long-term and short-term financial balances, reproductive capacity, indebtedness, maintaining the real value of equity, and opportunities to improve the financial position.

The tasks of the balance sheet analysis represent the concretization of the work that must be performed to achieve the goal of the analysis. Pre-set tasks greatly facilitate the achievement of the goal, because all jobs whose execution automatically achieves the goal of analysis are defined in advance. This frees the analyst from the dilemma of whether they have performed all the actions necessary to achieve the goal, and thus the dilemma of whether or not the goal of the analysis has been achieved.

However, for the tasks to be accurately defined and for some of the tasks not to be defined at all for setting tasks, it is necessary to have a comprehensive knowledge of potential factors that may affect the goal of the analysis. In other words, it means that it is not enough to know the method of analysis, but also all the factors that can influence either the appearance or the conditions.

Here's a sample balance sheet for a company below.

Assets	Amount	Liabilities	Amount
Current assets		**Short-term liabilities**	
Cash	300.000	Debts to creditors	2.000.000
Securities	100.000	Debts to suppliers	5.3000.000
Trade receivables	2.500.000	Other short-term liabilities	120.000
Stocks	1.000.000	**Total current liabilities**	7.420.000
Other current assets	490.000	Long-term loans	5.000.000
Total current assets	4.390.000	Other long-term liabilities	4.300.000
		Total liabilities	16.720.000
Fixed assets			
Buildings and equipment	14.000.000	**Share capital**	
Accumulated depreciation	7.800.000	Ordinary actions	4.000.000
Net fixed assets	6.200.000	Retained earnings	850.000
Intangible assets	8.996.000	**Total share capital**	4.850.000
Other assets	1.984.000		
Total assets	21.570.000	**Total liabilities**	21.570.000

In the example of the Balance Sheet, we can see that the company had 400 thousand cash and securities (300 plus 100), then receivables for goods sold of 2.5 million, which fell due. Inventories consist of materials and finished products waiting to be sold. A common feature of these assets, which are called current, is that in the near future they can be converted into money, unlike fixed assets (business premises, equipment, furniture, vehicles). According to the attached Balance Sheet, the gross value of fixed assets is 14 million. The present value of fixed assets is lowered by 7.8 million for depreciation, so it amounts to 6.2 million. Intangible assets amount to 8.9 million (projects, software, reputable business name, recognizable mark, brand, reputation of the company...) Then, if we compare the total current assets (4.39 million) and total short-term liabilities (7.42 million), it can be concluded that liabilities are higher than the value of assets by 3.03 million (4.39 - 7.42 = - 3.03). The value obtained is called Net Working Capital (NWC). There are also long-term liabilities, i.e. debts that need to be paid within a period of more than a year. The table shows that these liabilities amount to 5 million. Other long-term liabilities are 4.3 million.

At first sight, things that can raise concerns is the negative NWC and the relatively high liabilities. Negative net working capital is often a sign of a company's business problems, but that does not mean that the company is failing. Many large companies which have a negative working capital ratio and are doing well. Such companies can survive because they can quickly turn their assets into money and thus can meet their short-term obligations. They buy their stock from suppliers but sell it immediately.

Also, it is important to emphasize that there is no exact level of working capital that would be universally valid for all companies. The activity in which the company competes also plays a very important role in the management of working capital. E.g. for activities such as retail or catering it is not necessary to keep high levels of working capital as collection from customers is instantaneous and occurs daily when the company is doing business. In a relatively short period, it is possible to sell and collect all stocks of goods, and possibly part of fixed assets. In the case above, as the company is working in the trading sector, it can witness a lower value of NWC, especially in the first years of working. From the balance sheet, we can see that there is an ample amount of stock and a relatively high value of fixed assets.

However, if the case of negative or low NWC persists over a few years, this can be a warning sign that the company may need to change its strategy. Companies facing long-term negative net working capital may need to raise capital from investments, reduce costs, or raise prices.

Following is a presentation of the balance sheets of another company in the transportation industry. The balance sheets are for 4 years - 2016, 2017, 2018, and 2019.

	2016	2017	2018	2019
Fixed assets	17,211,032.93	13,412,706.59	3,452,102.33	287,401.11
Current assets	7,478,222.29	4,725,770.65	6,427,523.62	2,188,908.99
Loss above equity	/	/	3,980,942.86	8,907,724.89
Deferred expenses	286,334.21	194,099.55	235,938.57	7,760.50
ASSETS	24,975,589.43	18,332,576.79	14,096,507.38	11,391,795.49
Capital and reserves	16,019,556.31	4,261,626.74	/	/
Long-term provisions	/	4,471,337.92	7,456,894.34	6,173,963.83
Long-term	4,769,013.13	2,399,097.36	92,222.75	91,238.02
Short-term	4,187,019.99	7,200,514.77	6,547,390.29	5,126,593.64
LIABILITIES	24,975,589.43	18,332,576.79	14,096,507.38	11,391,795.49

At first glance, we notice that the condition of the assets shown in the balance sheet of this transport company is drastically deteriorating from year to year. A comparative balance sheet analysis will help us understand how negative business changes have occurred.

	2016.	2017.	Relation 2016-2017	Relation 2016-2017
			Amount of change	Percentage of change
Fixed assets	17,211.032,93	13,412.706,59	-3,798.326,34	-22,07
Current assets	7,478.222,29	4,725.770,65	-2,752.451,64	-36,81
Loss above the amount of capital	/	/	/	/
Deferred expenses	286.334,21	194.099,55	-92.234,66	-32,21
ASSETS	24,975.589,43	18,332.576,79	-6,643.012,64	-26,60
Capital and reserves	16,019.556,31	4,261.626,74	-11,757.929,57	-73,40
Long-term provisions	/	4,471.337,92	4,471.337,92	/
Long term obligations	4,769.013,13	2,399.097,36	-2,369.915,77	-49,69
Short-term liabilities	4,187.019,99	7,200.514,77	3,013.494,78	71,97
LIABILITIES	24,975.589,43	18,332.576,79	-6,643.012,64	-26,60

In the business year 2016, the company made a loss in the amount of 11,757,929.57, which harmed the balance of assets and capital.

	2018.	2019.	Relation 2019-2018	Relation 2019-2018
			Amount of change	Percentage of change
Fixed assets	3,452.102,33	287.401,11	-3,164.701,22	-91,67
Current assets	6,427.523,62	2,188.908,99	-4,238.614,63	-65,94
Loss above the amount of capital	3,980.942,86	8,907.724,89	4,926.782,03	123,76
Deferred expenses	235.935,57	7.760,50	-228.175,07	-96,71
ASSETS	14,096.507,38	11,391.795,49	-2,704.711,89	-19,19
Capital and reserves	/	/	/	/
Long-term provisions	7,456.894,34	6,173.963,83	-1,282.930,51	-17,20
Long term obligations	92.222,75	91.238,02	-984,73	-1,07
Short-term liabilities	6,547.390,29	5,126.593,64	-1,420.796,65	-21,70
LIABILITIES	14,096.507,38	11,391.795,49	2,704.711,89	-19,19

In the last observed period, we notice a continuation of the previous trend. The company is left with almost no fixed assets. If we know that its main activity is transportation, it is not difficult to understand that it has become impossible to continue performing the activity.

During the analysis of fixed assets, the structure of fixed assets, the present value, the spend and efficiency of using fixed assets are determined. Based on the analyzed parameters for the property position of the analyzed companies, it can be said that the first company presents a satisfactory case; and the second company, as already stated an unsatisfactory, or an unfavorable case as it is left with almost no fixed assets.

The indebtedness of the companies is examined by analyzing the liabilities of the balance sheet, from the aspect of ownership over the sources of financing. It is evident that the first company has a low risk of indebtedness as it got a sufficient amount of liabilities, while the other company is close to bankruptcy.

Although balance sheet analysis provides a basic insight into the state of the company (capital, assets, debt..), it is much better when this information is compared with the income statement and the ratio values.

CASH FLOW ANALYSIS

By including cash flow statements in a set of financial statements, new useful information for financial analysis is available to analysts. Cash flow is less able to be modified than profit. Given that the calculation of individual components of net profit involves accounting estimates, valuation, accruals, and allocations, it can be said that determining the net cash flow from operating activities is accompanied by a lower degree of subjectivity.

Financial indicators today are widely used analytical instruments used in assessing the performance of companies. Depending on what performance they measure, financial indicators can be grouped into indicators of liquidity, profitability, efficiency, financial leverage, and market indicators. This is a generally accepted division of financial indicators, but individual criteria and representatives of the mentioned groups may differ depending on the preferences of users and the understanding of their usefulness in a specific analysis.

All of them are interested in the information provided by the Cash Flow Report because they want to know what is happening with one of the most important resources of the company - cash. Therefore, this report will, in general, provide the following information to interested users:

1. Where the cash comes from during the reporting period,
2. How the cash was used during the period and
3. What changes occurred in the cash at the end compared to the beginning of the period

Information on the Cash Flow Statement helps users to:

- Assess the entity's ability to generate cash and cash equivalents and the entity's ability and needs to utilize those cash inflows;
- Assess the ability of the company to influence the amounts and timing of cash flows to adapt to changing opportunities and circumstances;
- Comparison of business activities of other companies, because cash flow excludes the possibility of using different accounting

methods for the same transactions and events related to business activities, so that balance sheet policy measures cannot, at least not directly, affect the amount of reported net cash flow.

The report on cash flows, providing information on the ratio of cash inflows and outflows, on the areas where cash inflows are realized and on the areas where cash needs are located, enables the management to identify the basic directions of its business activity when defining business policy. Based on the amount of realized net cash flow, the management formulates its dividend policy, and according to the sources of cash, it will determine the investment policy.

The Cash Flow Statement provides investors with the information necessary to:

- Assess the company's ability to manage cash equivalents,
- Assess the company's capacity to create positive incomes in the future
- Assess its ability to pay due liabilities,

- Assess its ability to pay dividends and interest;

- Created an opportunity to anticipate the need for additional funding.

The cash flow statement explains how from the cash balance at the beginning of the period - cash balance in the balance sheet of the previous period, to the cash balance at the end of the accounting period - cash balance in the balance sheet at the end of the current period. For this report, it is necessary, first of all, to define the basic categories of this report - cash and cash equivalents.

There are three basic understandings of cash:

- Narrowly understood cash - Money available for everyday use in the form of a legal mean of payment such as money in someone's wallet or cash register and current accounts of the company;

- Broadly understood cash - Which includes securities - securities purchased for resale or commercial purposes, and securities purchased for long-term investment (participation shares) and time deposits with banks;

- Cash equivalents - Items that can be quickly and easily converted into known amounts of money but are in themselves neither 'narrowly understood cash' nor 'broadly understood cash'. Cash equivalents include those securities that are not purchased for resale or long-term investment of free funds. The most common cash equivalents are government bonds, government bills, etc.

Cash inflows may occur due to:

- An increase in liabilities (liabilities or equity based on the owner's payment) or
- A decrease in non-cash assets (by converting tangible or intangible assets through write-offs to cash, for example).

Cash outflows occur:

- By reducing liabilities (by settling liabilities or withdrawing capital by the owner) or
- By increasing asset positions other than cash (by investing in tangible, intangible, and other forms of assets other than cash).

All activities of the company are aimed at creating value for owners and creditors. Creating value for owners and creditors is the primary goal, but it cannot be achieved without creating value for consumers. Therefore, the primary goal - the realization of value for owners and creditors is achieved by the realization of the latter.

All cash flows that the company realizes can occur as:

- Cash flows from business (operational) activities,
- Cash flows from investing activities and
- Cash flows from financial activities.

This classification of activities enables the users of the Cash Flow Statement to:

- Assess the impact of these activities on the financial position of the company and
- Assess the relationship between the activities themselves.

Therefore, based on these activities, the share of cash inflows and outflows and cash equivalents of individual groups of activities in the total business is assessed. This assessment is used to determine the

36

contribution of individual activities to the overall financial result is estimated. From the information on the net cash flow, it can be seen which activities had a positive, and which a negative effect on the final cash balance at the end of the period.

CASH FLOWS FROM OPERATING ACTIVITIES

Cash flows from operating activities arise primarily from the principal activities of revenue-generating enterprises. The statement of cash flows from operating activities marks the degree to which the organization's activities have produced adequate money inflows to keep the business functioning. Business activities are the main activities of entrepreneurs arising from transactions and business events that determine or affect profit or loss.

The measure of incomes emerging from operating activities is a key marker of the degree to which the company has created adequate incomes to reimburse credits, keep up business functions, deliver profits and make new ventures without utilizing outer financing means. Information about specific elements of past operating cash flows is useful, along with other information, in forecasting future cash flows from operating activities.

CASH FLOWS FROM INVESTMENT ACTIVITIES

Investment activities include receipts and expenditures related to transactions with fixed assets, i.e., acquisition and disposal of fixed assets and other investments, which are not included in cash equivalents. It is important to disclose separately the cash flows arising from investing activities, as they reflect the amount of expenditures incurred for resources intended to generate future profits and cash flows.

CASH FLOWS FROM FINANCIAL ACTIVITIES

Cash flows from financing activities show the cash transactions of an enterprise with its owners and transactions with creditors who borrow money. Financial activities are those that determine the capital owned by the company, as well as its lending condition.

Entities that provide equity to the company in any way are particularly interested in cash flows arising from financing activities. It is important to emphasize that financial cash flows include borrowings and repayment of long-term and short-term loans, but not interest paid on loans that are recorded as cash flows from operating activities.

The following examples show direct and indirect method calculations of cash flow.

Cash flow statement - indirect method

Cash flows from operating activities	
Profit before tax and extraordinary items	10.500
Adjustments for:	
Depreciation	500
Operating profit before changes in working capital	11.000
Increases in receivables	(4.500)
Stock reduction	3.000
Increase in operating liabilities (suppliers)	2,000
Net cash flow from operating activities	11.500
Cash flows from investing activities	
Cash receipts from sale of long-term investments	1.000
Cash outflows for the purchase of equipment	(2.000)
Net cash flow from investing activities	(1.000)
Cash flows from financing activities	
Receipts from issue of shares	2.000
Expenditures for repayment of part of the loan principal	(1.000)
Net cash flow from financing activities	1.000
NET CASH FLOW	11.500
Cash and cash equivalents at the beginning of the period	11.500
Cash and cash equivalents at the end of the period	23.000
INCREASE IN MONEY	11.500

Cash flow statement - direct method

Cash flows from operating activities	
Receipts from collection of receivables	64.500
Expenditures for paid liabilities to suppliers	(53.000)
Net cash flow from operating activities	11.500
Cash flows from investing activities	
Cash receipts from sale of long-term investments	1.000
Cash outflows for the purchase of equipment	(2.000)
Net cash flow from investing activities	(1.000)
Cash flows from financing activities	
Receipts from issue of shares	2.000
Expenditures for repayment of part of the loan principal	(1.000)
Net cash flow from financing activities	1.000
NET CASH FLOW	11.500
Cash and cash equivalents at the beginning of the period	11.500
Cash and cash equivalents at the end of the period	23.000
INCREASE IN MONEY	11.500

In the case of the direct method, total receipts and total expenditures are classified into business, investment, and financial activities to calculate the net cash flow.

For the indirect method, net cash flows from operating activities are determined using a different method. It is calculated by adjusting the net profit or net loss for the effects of changes in inventories, receivables, liabilities, non-cash items (depreciation, provisions, deferred taxes) and all other activities that cause cash flows from investment and financing activities.

Cash flows created by the direct method provide more reliable information and are more understandable to users. Therefore, it is recommended to use the direct method.

VALUATION RATIOS

The relationships between quantities as instruments of quantitative analysis are in fact comparison of one quantity with another. In this case, a relationship between two quantities that have the same characteristics but appeared in two different times can be established. This expresses the dynamics of a phenomenon or state. On the other hand, there is a relationship between two quantities that have different characteristics or features but are interdependent, one conditioning the other. This expresses the degree of conditionality. However, regardless of that, the ratios of sizes can be expressed: by scale, coefficient, index, and percentage.

Scale. A scale is reached if two or more quantities expressed in absolute numbers are shortened by the same numbers to the extent that it is no longer possible to perform further shortening.

Coefficient. The coefficient (often called ratio in the literature) is reached if one quantity is divided by another and thus expresses the ratio of these quantities, which, represents the relative magnitude of their conditionality.

Index. An index is a ratio of two quantities that shows their relative change (variation), in a certain period. For time series, the index can be fixed base and chain. In the first case, the magnitude of the first period is taken as a basis of all subsequent periods. In the second case, the size of each previous period is taken as a basis of the size of the next period.

Percentage. A percentage is an expression of a relative change in percentages. If the change is measured in two periods, the value from the previous period is taken as 100 as the base, and the size of the next period expresses an increase or decrease compared to 100.

Valuation Ratios

Ratio is a relative number obtained between one balance value and another. In doing so, it should be borne in mind that the relationship should include quantities that are interrelated or conditioned. Ratio indicators are the carriers of information needed to make decisions about managing a company.

Indicators are calculated and used depending on the interests of business decision-makers. Thus, e.g., capital owners are interested in long-term profitability and security; lenders are interested in liquidity indicators. The company's management is interested in all business indicators because it cares about liquidity, short-term, and long-term financial stability and profitability.

Ratio indicators are grouped as:

1. Liquidity indicators

2. Leverage indicators

3. Turnover indicators

4. Economic indicators

5. Profitability indicators

6. Investment indicators

Liquidity and leverage indicators can be viewed as indicators of business security. Indicators of turnover, economy, and profitability are indicators of business success (efficiency). The relationship between these indicators is not straightforward, but they are all interconnected because success provides security in the long run and vice versa.

Liquidity ratios

Liquidity as a concept can be analyzed from two aspects, namely the liquidity of assets and the liquidity of the company. The liquidity of an asset that is in non-monetary form represents its ability to transform into monetary form. The time required for this transformation determines the degree of liquidity of the observed non-cash asset. In this case, it is about the liquidity of a non-monetary asset.

When liquidity is viewed as the performance of a business entity, then it is defined differently. Liquidity includes three important elements - time limit, means of payment, and financial obligation. Quantitative, i.e. value and time harmonization of these elements is a necessary condition for achieving and maintaining the liquidity of the company. Viewed from this aspect, liquidity can be described as the financial balance of the company, given that the financial balance of the company implies that the monetary expenditures that the company must make at a certain time are covered by its cash income.

Therefore, with the financial balance, the company provides the ability to settle its obligations within a certain period, i.e. on time and in full amount without any restrictions regarding these parameters.

Liquidity is one of the basic requirements that is crucial for management, and it is generated by the requirements of external factors, i.e. creditors. Liquidity ratios are calculated by relating certain values contained in balance sheet items. Depending on the quantities included in the relationship, liquidity indicators can be classified by cash, quick, current, and financial stability.

The **cash liquidity ratio** is calculated as cash and cash equivalents divided by short-term liabilities. If the funds available to the business entity are equal to or greater than the obligations, then it can be said that the company is considered liquid. In this case, the calculated coefficient would be 1 or greater than 1 which is the preferred condition. However, this indicator is not a guarantee of maintaining liquidity in the future, so it is necessary to calculate other ratios.

Another important liquidity ratio is the **quick liquidity**, which is calculated as follows: (cash and cash equivalents + short-term receivables

)/ short-term liabilities. This ratio should also be 1 or higher than 1, but not too high because it would indicate a high level of cash that would require changes in terms of improving cash management and changing credit policy.

The **current liquidity ratio** is one of the most commonly used indicators. It is equal to current assets / short-term liabilities. For current liquidity to be at a satisfactory level, its ratio needs to be 2, which means that the ratio of short-term sources and short-term liabilities should be 2: 1. This requirement arises from the fact that there are risks that a certain part of current assets will not be able to be liquidated immediately.

Such reserves are established keeping in mind that current sources consist of cash, short-term securities, receivables, and inventories. In all of them, except for the cash part, there is a risk of collection both on time and in full amount. Therefore, to provide current liquidity, it is necessary, and in practice, this is often the case, that part of short-term funds are financed from long-term sources. This part of quality long-term sources is called working capital and is determined as the difference between current assets and short-term liabilities. Therefore, working capital shows how much short-term assets are financed from quality long-term sources.

The **coefficient of financial stability** = long-term tied assets / (capital + long-term liabilities + long-term provisions). It should be less than 1. If this coefficient is less than 1, it means that all fixed assets are financed with long-term sources and that part of long-term sources is used to finance short-term assets. In practice, this means that the company meets the need for working capital and that the conditions for financial stability of the company are provided.

Liquidity is a variable category that is influenced by many internal and external factors. Having in mind its importance for maintaining good business relations with creditors, which is a condition for uninterrupted and continuous business, it must be approached in a planned manner with continuous verification of its coefficients.

Although the liquidity of the company is closely related to the liquidity of the assets at the disposal of the company, the two should not be equated in any way. Company liquidity is a category that has its own dynamics that depend, above all, on the inflow and outflow of funds, which is why the management must pay special attention to the harmonization of monetary movements.

Leverage indicators

To finance its business, the company uses various sources from which it provides the necessary financial resources. First of all, business entities use their funds to finance business activities. However, in practice, often funds from own sources are not sufficient, so the management is necessarily instructed to find external sources to finance business activities. Thus, business entities enter into debt relations by borrowing funds for the smooth running of business processes.

Having in mind that the borrowed funds must be repaid on time with the corresponding interest as the price of the borrowed capital, for the management and the creditors, i.e. lenders, it is important to know whether that company can repay the debt.

Precisely these reasons impose the need for an analysis of financial security, i.e. the level of indebtedness of the company. These indicators are calculated based on information from the balance sheet and essentially show the relationship between own and other people's sources of financing, i.e. indicate the financial structure of the company. They are also called leverage indicators in the literature.

Solvency means the ability of a company to settle all its liabilities with total funds, assuming that they all fall due on the same day. The solvency of a company essentially represents liquidity in the long run, which means that it can fulfill all its obligations within the deadlines in which they mature. It is often the case that a company can fulfill its short-term obligations, i.e. that it is liquid, but in the long run, it will not be able to fulfill long-term obligations upon their maturity, which means that it is insolvent.

The insolvency of the company is caused by excessive borrowing as a consequence of conducting an inadequate financial policy of the company. Therefore, the management must often check the solvency, i.e. financial stability with the help of ratio indicators.

Indebtedness indicators can be different depending on what they need to present, the most common of which are the following: debt, net-working capital, financing, coverage of interest expenses ratio.

A higher level of **debt ratio** (total liabilities/total assets) also means a higher risk of investing in companies. It should not be higher than 0.5 and preferably smaller, which means that the share of liabilities in relation to total assets is 50%.

The **financing ratio** is calculated as total liabilities/working capital. Taking into account modern business conditions, many banks, when approving a loan, require that this ratio be 2: 1, which represents the limit of the company's creditworthiness.

This coverage of interest expenses indicator (total liabilities/retained earnings + depreciation) is often used by banks and other financial institutions when considering business applications for loans. This is how they assess the ability of a company to meet interest costs for a possible loan. This indicator checks whether the company has achieved a business that has provided a profit sufficient to easily cover interest costs, or the costs are too high to cover them without jeopardizing the size of profits, and thus part of the profit available for dividends on ordinary shares.

Turnover (activity)

Through the process of activities, the company strives to use the available funds as effectively as possible, i.e. to achieve the largest possible volume of activities with the least possible investment in funds (minimax principle). The measure of that effectiveness is obtained from the relationship between the realized volume of activities (i.e. income or expenditure as a financial expression of the quantity and range of products produced and sold) and investment in business assets.

Indicators resulting from this relationship are referred to as activity indicators or performance indicators. This group of indicators provides an answer to the question of how effectively the company uses the available funds and is the basis for assessing whether the balance sheet assets correspond to the amount of realized (planned) revenues.

Determining and controlling activity indicators is of great importance from the aspect of company financial management because the relations between effects and investments directly determine the degree of liquidity and profitability of the company. Although activity indicators (turnover ratios) can be defined for each category of business assets of the company, few are commonly used, as follows:

Customer turnover ratio (Net sales revenue/ average number of customers) – Without going into the factors that determine the worth of receivables from customers, from the aspect of maintaining the company's ability to pay, it is very important to anticipate the time in which receivables are converted into cash. As a generally accepted method for testing the convertibility of receivables in cash, the customer turnover ratio and average collection period are used.

In companies where investments in inventories make up a significant portion in the structure of assets, testing the convertibility of inventories into cash is very important. The inventory turnover ratio = costs of materials / average inventories. Since the position of inventories includes assets in different phases of the operation process, they are usually differentiated into pre-production inventories (raw materials), inventories in the production process (work in progress and semi-finished products), and inventories of finished products.

From the aspect of maintaining liquidity and managing cash flows, it is very important to know the average time in which short-term liabilities are due. The **supplier turnover ratio** is usually used for these purposes.

Since the number of annual purchases of materials and services on credit does not appear in the income statement, it can be determined in two ways:

- Determining the exact amount based on a review of accounting documentation on the procurement, which is a complicated and long process and available only to analysts in the company

- By approximating the value of annual purchases of materials and services on credit based on data contained in the positions of the balance sheet and income statement. The usual approximation of that amount is obtained by adjusting the cost price of sold products to change the balance on the inventory account. The principle is that the increase in inventories at the end of the period compared to the opening balance is added, and the decrease is deducted from the cost price of products sold

55

Fixed assets in many companies take the largest part of business assets (65-70%), which is why it is very important to control the efficiency of their use. This is the turnover ratio of current assets = sales revenue / average value of current assets. This indicator is estimated in the context of normal values from previous accounting periods or is compared with indicators of related companies or the average for the branch to which the company belongs. The reasons for unfavorable (low) value should be sought either in excessive investments in fixed assets (insufficient capacity utilization) or in the unfavorable structure of those assets. Such situations are common in companies with an oversized non-productive component of fixed assets (e.g. real estate). It is a reasonable recommendation that the reasons for low value must be examined in detail, given that, due to the amount of investment, fixed assets significantly affect the profitability and liquidity of the company.

Total business assets represent the total economic power that the company has at its disposal for the process of activities. Since, in financial terms, the level of business activity is reflected in the realized operating income during a certain period, then it is logical that the level of operating income expresses the efficiency of using the total operating assets of the company. This is represented by the turnover ratio of total assets = total income / average value of assets. Since the calculation of this ratio includes the total available business assets of the company, it is the most general indicator of the efficiency of use of business assets of the company and, accordingly, integrates and summarizes the turnover ratios of certain categories of assets (receivables, inventories, fixed assets). The interest of the company is to increase the efficiency of the use of business assets (maximizing this ratio), which is objectively limited by the possibilities of maximizing the turnover of certain categories of assets.

Economic (cost-effectiveness) indicators

To carry out business activities, the company must provide various resources as a prerequisite for starting a business process. The necessary elements for every business process are objects of labor, means of labor and labor itself, or workforce. These elements are consumed during the business process and transfer their value to the newly created business performance, i.e. product or service. This is how the company's expenses are incurred. By realizing the newly created business effects, the company generates revenues. The goal of every business is to keep the expenses incurred during the production of effects as low as possible, and the revenues generated by the realization of these effects as high as possible. Precisely this business principle, which strives to achieve the highest possible income per unit of expenditure, is called economy of business.

The essence of the principle of economy is in saving the components of production in the business process of the company. Due to the importance of economy as one of the basic target principles of business of every company, its analysis, i.e. calculation of indicators of economy is a necessary prerequisite for understanding the condition and success of each business entity.

Thus, business efficiency is a certain relationship between income and expenses, and the information contained in the income statement is used to calculate these indicators. Economic indicators can be grouped depending on which categories of income and expenses are used in relation to each other. The most commonly used cost-effectiveness indicators are **cost-effectiveness of overall business, cost-effectiveness of sales, and cost-effectiveness of financing**.

Profitability indicators:

Profitability expresses the effectiveness of the use (earning power) of assets (invested capital). The degree of earning power is considered an expression of the company's ability to generate new value, which is the goal of financial management. In the financial sense, the ability to generate new value is equated with the financial condition of the company, i.e. the primary security of the interests of the owners and creditors of the company.

Namely, investors and creditors will find it difficult to decide on investments in a company whose return on invested capital is minimal, because it does not provide enough guarantees that the obligations based on the engaged capital will be paid in full and on time. To assess the earning power of the company, a special group of efficiency indicators has been developed, which look at the effects of activities in relation to the level of sales revenue or compared to the funds invested in their acquisition.

The aim of this analysis is to find answers to two key questions: 1. What part of each monetary unit of sales revenue represents profit? 2. How much profit does each monetary unit of engaged business assets bring? The answer to the first question is given by the analysis of the ratio of realized profit and sales revenue from the income statement, through the indicator of the profit rate (yield margin). The answer to the second question is given by indicators of rate of return (global profitability indicators), which are determined from the relationship between the effects of activities and the categories of assets by which they are generated.

The income statement for the purposes of profit rate analysis must be structured so that revenues and expenses are presented segmented (by types, functional units, markets, etc.). The goal is to gradually cover the segment of sales revenue segment by expense segment (costs of products sold, period costs, interest, and taxes) to:

- Obtain intermediate results of activities of different levels (gross profit, operating profit, profit before and after-tax, and net profit)

- Consideration of the share and contribution of each segment of expenses to the achieved business result.

The reasons for such an approach are purely pragmatic because covering all expenditures from periodic revenues would make it impossible to control certain segments of total costs and intermediate results. Such control aims to keep the variable components of individual cost segments in direct proportion to the scope of activities while maintaining the fixed components at a relatively constant level or translating them into a zone of degression.

In principle, the growth of the profit rate indicator (net profit, gross and operating margin) means a positive tendency, in terms of widening the range between income and expenditure. An analysis of the movement of individual rates (margins) over several consecutive years can give a fairly decent insight into the company's operations in that period. The stability of gross profit margin during the observed period, with a simultaneous decline in net profit margin, is a reliable indicator of the growth of period costs, financing, or tax rates. This points to the need for a more detailed analysis of these categories to see the causes of such movements.

Investment indicators

Market value indicators, unlike other groups of indicators that rely only on the data contained in the financial statements, use information from the financial market. The most important information from that market is the market price of the shares of a particular company (provided that the shares are listed on the stock exchange), which expresses the prevailing price at which one share is sold or bought at a certain time.

Provided that the capital market is efficient, then the product of the number of issued shares of the company and the current market price of the shares expresses the market value of the company. Data on market prices of individual shares, together with other relevant data, are published publicly in a specialized stock exchange and other publications.

Market value indicators should provide an answer to the question: Do business owners (shareholders) receive an adequate return on their investment? From the shareholders' point of view, owning shares makes sense only if the capital invested in their purchase brings a return, either through dividends or through the growth of the market price of shares. The amount of dividend per share means the annual income of shareholders per one share and is expressed in absolute monetary amount. The data on the annual dividend per share is obtained by simply dividing the part of net profit determined for the payment of dividends to shareholders and the number of ordinary shares (for previous periods) or based on declared dividends (planned for payment), which companies usually publish quarterly. The data on net profit per share from the aspect of current or potential shareholders is not very relevant, because the amount of dividend per share, in addition to the amount of realized net profit, is also determined by distribution decisions.

Some common indicators are earnings per share, dividend per share, return on shares, price-earnings per share, price-to-share, ratio of price and book value of a share, price-to-cash-flow ratio per share, and so on.

The indicators presented so far do not mean much by themselves. For the analyst or decision-maker, indicators will matter when compared. Indicators can be compared:

- With the planned in the company
- With the planned in the environment
- With the achieved indicators in a certain period of the company or environment
- With the average indicators of the company or branch

Now that we defined valuation ratios, we are going to show their application through an example of a company with the following balance sheet:

	Amount in 1000s		Structure %		
	Current year	Previous year	Current year	Previous year	Index
ASSETS	103,592	97,948	9.64%	9.92%	105.72
A. FIXED ASSETS (I to V)			0.00%	0.00%	0
I. UNPAID SUBSCRIBED CAPITAL			0.00%	0.00%	0
II. GOODWILL			0.00%	0.00%	0
III. INTANGIBLE INVESTMENTS	103,592	97,648	9.64%	9.89%	106.08
IV. REAL ESTATE, PLANTS, EQUIPMENT AND BIOLOGICAL ASSETS (1 + 2 + 3)	89,242	92,832	8.31%	9.40%	96.132
1. Real estate plant and equipment			0.00%	0.00%	0
2. Investment real estate			0.00%	0.00%	0
3 Biological agents	0	300	0.00%	0.03%	0
V. LONG-TERM FINANCIAL INVESTMENTS (1 + 2)			0.00%	0.00%	0
1. Participation in capital		300	0.00%	0.03%	0
2. Other long-term placements	970,692	889,571	90.36%	90.08%	109.11
B. CURRENT ASSETS (I TO IV)	527,444	491,503	49.10%	49.77%	107.31
I. INVENTORIES	40,511	48,720	3.771%	4.934%	83.150
II. FIXED ASSETS FOR SALE AND ASSETS FROM DISCONTINUED OPERATIONS	402,737	349,348	37.49%	35.38%	115.28
III. SHORT-TERM RECEIVABLES, PLACEMENTS AND CASH (1 to 5)	171,510	158,501	15.97%	16.05%	108.20
1. Receivables	3,701		0.34%	0.00%	0
2. Receivables for overpaid income tax	183,779	153,672	17.11%	15.56%	119.59
3. Short-term financial investments	40,410	23,973	3.76%	2.43%	168.56
4. Cash equivalents and cash	103,592	97,948	9.64%	9.92%	105.72
5. Value added tax and accruals	3,337	13,202	0.31%	1.34%	25.276
IV. DEFERRED TAX ASSETS			0.00%	0.00%	0
C. BUSINESS ASSETS (A + B)	1,074,284	987,519	100.00%	100.0%	108.78
D. LOSS OVER CAPITAL			0.00%	0.00%	0
E. TOTAL ASSETS (C + D)	1,074,284	987,519	100.00%	100.0%	108.78

F. OFF-BALANCE SHEET ASSETS					0
LIABILITIES					
A. CAPITAL (I + II + III + IV + V-VI + VII-VIII-IX)	1,060,631	964,893	98.73%	97.73%	109.92
I. SHARE AND OTHER CAPITAL	497,369	497,359	46.30%	50.38%	100.00
II. UNPAID SHARE CAPITAL			0.00%	0.00%	0
III. RESERVES			0.00%	0.00%	0
IV. REVALUATION RESERVES			0.00%	0.00%	0
V. UNREALIZED GAINS ON SECURITIES			0.00%	0.00%	0
VI. UNREALIZED LOSSES ON THE BASIS OF VALUES			0.00%	0.00%	0
VII. RETAINED EARNINGS	563,262	467,534	52.43%	47.36%	120.47
VIII. LOSS			0.00%	0.00%	0
IX. OWNED OWN SHARES			0.00%	0.00%	0
B. LONG-TERM PROVISIONS AND LIABILITIES (I TO IV)	13,633	22,402	1.27%	2.27%	60.856
I. LONG - TERM PROVISIONS	11,000	10,500	1.02%	1.06%	104.76
II. LONG-TERM LIABILITIES (1 + 2)			0.00%	0.00%	0
1. Long-term loans			0.00%	0.00%	0
2. other long-term liabilities			0.00%	0.00%	0
III. SHORT-TERM LIABILITIES (1 to 6)	2,633	11,902	0.25%	1.21%	22.122
1. Short-term financial liabilities		483	0.00%	0.05%	0
2. Liabilities based on assets held for sale and assets of discontinued operations			0.00%	0.00%	0
3. Operating liabilities	1,960	9,357	0.18%	0.95%	20.946
4. Other short-term liabilities	585	664	0.05%	0.07%	88.102
5. Liabilities based on value added tax, other public revenues and accrued costs and deferred revenue	88	186	0.01%	0.02%	47.311
6. Income tax liabilities		1,212	0.00%	0.12%	0
IV. DEFERRED TAX LIABILITIES	20	224	0.00%	0.02%	8.9285
C. TOTAL LIABILITIES (A + B)	1,074,264	987,295	100.00%	100.0%	108.80
D. OFF-BALANCE SHEET LIABILITIES	28,595	21,506			132.96

Type of coefficient	Current year	Previous year	Ref. value
Liquidity ratios			
Cash ratio	15.348	2.014	>1
Quick liquidity ratio	81.892	15.331	>=1
Current liquidity ratio	368.664	74.741	>=2
Coefficient of financial stability	0.589	0.604	<1
Solvency ratio	78.80	44.08	
Leverage ratios			
Financial leverage ratio	0.012854	0.023217	
Self-financing ratio	0.462977	0.503645	Min 0.5
Indebtedness ratio	0.023706	2.069832	
Economic (cost-effectiveness) ratios			
An indicator of the economy of overall business	1.242467	1.313693	>1
Business regularity indicator	1.2579	1.31419	>1
Funding indicator	1.044082	21.67422	>1
Turnover ratios			
Rate of return on total capital	0.164479	0.196429	Higher the better
Return on equity	0.269095	0.390302	
Profitability			
Net Profit Margin	0.035585	0.219916	>1
Gross profit margin	0.230725	0.238784	
Net return on assets	0.151583	0	
Investment ratios			
Earnings per share	892.2533	1294.147	
Dividend per share			
Profitability of the action			

The cash liquidity ratio represents the ability of the company to settle liabilities that are due from the distribution of cash and cash equivalents. In the case of the observed company, this ratio, as well as other liquidity ratios, shows a tendency to increase in the current compared to the previous year, and thus the company is more liquid. The company is also solvent, which is attributed to the rapid growth of business assets in relation to the company's liabilities.

Indebtedness ratios show that the dynamics of financial leverage are declining, which shows that liabilities are decreasing in relation to capital and thus the indebtedness of the company is decreasing.

When it comes to the coefficient of own financing, it is slightly lower in the current year compared to the previous year. This coefficient should be at least 0.5, and if it is not so, the level of self-financing decreases because the level of creditor security is lower and the business risk of the company increases.

The indebtedness ratio should always be as low as possible because it shows how long it takes a company to settle its obligations. In the example above, this coefficient is significantly reduced in the current compared to the previous year and amounts to just 0.024.

The economy of the company, based on the results, is solid in both observed years, although in the current year it is lower than in the previous one because the costs grow faster than the revenues.

When it comes to financing indicators, we see that in both observed years the reference value was met, i.e. the coefficient is> 1, but the coefficient decreased significantly in the current year compared to the previous year.

The rate of return on total capital decreases in the current compared to the previous year because a lower return is realized on the same capital.

The profitability indicator is also declining in the current year, and this ratio shows the company's ability to earn in relation to shareholders' investments. This means that the return on equity is reduced.

The net profit margin shows the final effect, ie what the effects are, by the growth of realization. In the observed company, the dynamics of the net margin decreases because a smaller profit is allocated to a higher realized income.

The gross profit margin shows the share of gross profit in the total sales of the company. In the observed company, it decreases because the total income grows, but a lower gross profit and gross profit margin stand out.

In summary, the company's profits are reduced this year due to an increase in expenses. However, the profits of the company have been put to good use as the company has higher liquidity and lower indebtedness this year.

MANAGEMENT OF ASSETS (DEPRECIATION AND AMORTIZATION)

Assets are controlled resources. Companies expect an inflow of economic benefit from them, as a result of past events. Assets have the potential to contribute, directly or indirectly, to the inflow of cash and cash equivalents. Future economic benefits, embodied in assets, cash flow to the company in several ways.

Fixed assets have a constant appearance of form and, as a rule, are not intended for sale but use in the business process. It is expected to be realized in cash over more than one year or for a period longer than the duration of the business cycle so that the money is generally long engaged in such forms of assets. Sometimes the period of use is extremely long (e.g. office buildings, sales premises) and can be up to 50, 100 years or longer. Related to the permanence of the phenomenon is the fact that fixed assets will not be consumed at once, once in one production cycle or one period, but are entered in unchanged form in several production cycles or periods.

71

The specificity of the consumption of fixed assets is expressed through the calculation of depreciation and amortization. The term defines the gradual depreciation of fixed assets, where the value spent appears as an integral part of the value of products or services. This is achieved by including the used (expanded) part of fixed assets as the cost of depreciation in the cost of production of the product or the cost of the service provided.

With the sale of products or services (charging of claims), part of the amortization is converted, i.e. returned into cash.

The use of assets in business is related to its gradual use of economic benefits and therefore it is necessary to allocate the total depreciation amount (total amount recognized as depreciation expense over the life of the asset) to individual years in use according to the use of assets in certain years of its life use. This is done to enable the most objective confrontation of depreciation as an expense with the realized income.

The basis for calculating depreciation, which can be defined as the cost of acquisition of assets less than the residual value, is called the depreciation amount. The estimated amount that an entity would currently receive by disposing of an asset after deducting the estimated disposal costs is called the residual value but provided that the age of the asset and condition correspond to those expected at the end of its useful life. That is, it is the amount expected to be realized from the sale of the asset at the end of its estimated useful life. The amount of the residual value reduces the cost of acquisition of the asset when determining the basis for calculating depreciation.

Therefore, determining the amount of depreciation expense is based on:

- Depreciation amount
- Depreciation period or the estimated amount of effects in the useful life of depreciable assets
- Annual depreciation rates
- Depreciation system and depreciation method

Characteristics of depreciable assets:

- Intended for use in the manufacture or sale of products, goods, or services, for rent to others or administrative purposes

- Are expected to be used for more than one billing period

- Have a limited service life.

Since the consumption of economic benefits begins from the beginning of the use of the property, that is when the depreciation begins. In practice, depreciation usually begins to accrue from the first day of the month following the month in which the asset is put into use. Assets that are subject to depreciation are depreciated over their entire useful lives. In the case when a certain asset is temporarily out of use (e.g. due to relocation), the calculation of depreciation usually does not stop.

The basis for calculating depreciation is the total depreciation cost over the entire estimated useful life of the asset. Each depreciation method will result in the same total amount of depreciation expense over the entire estimated useful life of the asset, but the annual depreciation amounts in individual years of the estimated useful life of a particular asset will differ. The basis for the calculation of depreciation may be determined in the amount of the cost of acquisition of assets, the cost of acquisition less the residual value, the revalued amount, or the revalued amount less the residual value.

There are three depreciation methods, and they are:

1. Proportional or linear method

2. Degressive method

3. Progressive method

The proportional or linear method is the simplest method of depreciation and the most commonly used method in accounting. With this method, it is specified that the depreciation rate and the annual depreciation amounts are the same throughout the estimated useful life of the assets. The determined depreciation rate is constant for the entire estimated useful life.

- Example: Calculation of annual depreciation, by the linear method, for an office equipment with a purchase value of 80.000, and an estimated useful life of 5 years.

Depreciation = 80.000 * (100: 5)% = 80.000 * 20% = 16.000

The degressive depreciation method is a form of time depreciation method in which the rate of depreciation in the first years of life is higher and then gradually decreases over its useful life. In the first year, the amount of depreciation is the highest, and in the last year the lowest. This method also determines the depreciation rates for each year of service life.

Example

Calculation of depreciation, using the degressive method, for a car with a purchase value of 100.000, and an estimated residual value of 10.000. The estimated useful life is 60,000 km.

The amount of depreciation per kilometer is obtained as follows: (100.000 – 10.000): 60,000 km = 1.5 depreciation per kilometer. At the end of each year, the amount of depreciation will be determined by multiplying the rate by 150% by the number of kilometers the car has traveled during the year. The car, after covering 60.000 km, is fully depreciated and depreciation stops. It is assumed that the car passes 25.000 km in the first year, 15.000 km in the second year, 12.000 km in the third year, and 8.000 km in the fourth year:

Year of car use	Mileage	Depreciation expense	Accumulated depreciation	Book value
I.	25.000	37.500	37.500	62.500
II.	15.000	22.500	60.000	40.000
III.	12.000	18.000	78.000	22.000
IV.	8.000	12.000	90.000	10.000
Total	60.000	90.000		

The progressive depreciation method is the opposite of the degressive method. With this method, the amount of depreciation is lower in the first years of use and then gradually increases over the useful life. The progressive depreciation method is applied in case when a certain asset is used with less intensity in the first years of its useful life, and over the years, the intensity of exploitation gradually increases.

Example

Calculation of depreciation, using the progressive method, for a property with a value of 250,000, and the depreciation period of 4 years.

The depreciation rate is lowest in the first year and highest in the last. Also, the write-off percentage rate is continuously growing from the lowest to the highest year (5% -40%)

Year	Purchase value	Write-off rate	Basis of calculation	Depreciation costs	Accumulated depreciation	Present (unwritten) value
0	250.000					250.000
1		5%	250.000	12.500	12.500	237.500
2		20%	250.000	50.000	62.500	187.500
3		35%	250.000	87.500	150.000	100.000
4		40%	250.000	100.000	250.000	-

CRITICAL METRICS TO ANALYZE GROWTH

Employees, managers, investors, and policymakers strive to understand company growth so that they can make better investment decisions, be better employees, managers, or offer economic policies that drive company growth. The enterprise as such is a very complex mechanism with clear aspirations and goals of creating wealth and profit from the very beginning of existence.

Defining economic growth and development is far simpler than defining enterprise growth and development. Economic growth is measured by gross national product and it is a consequence of the actions of actors that make such decisions and affect economic development. The growth of a company is not so easy to define as every part of the company may grow, but their growth is not harmonized and is not reflected in the development of the company.

Company growth can be measured in different ways, as there are several indicators in which growth can be expressed. To measure the growth of a company means to choose the type of economic phenomenon that will represent growth, choose the method of measurement, means, and type of measure by which it will be measured, and finally carry out the measurement process itself.

5 year Revenue

In most cases, revenue projection is made separately for individual sources. This step is extremely important because each source has its own rules by which it operates. Breaking down larger revenue items into smaller ones will reduce errors. By breaking down income into the simplest items, errors can also be minimized by canceling the plus and minus errors by individual positions.

Companies need to focus on the sources that bring the most revenue to the budget. Therefore, the projection must be as accurate as possible, while, on the other hand, it is of little use to work hard to estimate revenues from sources that bring minimal revenues because they do not have a greater impact on the overall budget.

Data from previous years is used to determine the upward or downward trend of revenues or expenditures. Data from previous years are important but not the only data needed to create an income projection. This information is usually the total amount of income data from previous years, based on which it is possible to determine the trend. Then, occasional or irregular fluctuations in revenues and expenditures within each source should be considered. This aspect is of particular importance.

In completely mathematical calculation, the method of predicting the future trend is accepted, the so-called least-squares method, which will be discussed below. It serves for the analysis of the so-called "historical", trends in changes in revenues and expenditures from individual sources, and their continuation in the future.

Determining the trend line, according to this analysis, enables the prediction of future revenues and expenses. Determining the trend enables the preparation of a future projection and possibly further calculations. With the help of samples, trends from the past are "transmitted" through the calculation process in the next 5 years. In further analyzes, the management can accept the assumptions for the projections in three versions: baseline, pessimistic, and optimistic, and make those versions. After careful consideration, one of the specially calculated versions should eventually be accepted to get a certain prediction of the future of revenues.

We are going to use the case of a company in the fitness business to show how revenue projections are composed.

	REVENUE ITEMS	REVENUES DURING THE OBSERVED YEARS OF OPERATION (QUANTITY X PRICES)					TOTAL
		Year 1	Year 2	Year 3	Year 4	Year 5	
I.	PRODUCT OFFERING						
II.	SALE OF GOODS	120.000,00	144.100,00	187.500,00	233.100,00	278.150,00	962.850,00
1.	Food products	120.000,00	144.100,00	187.500,00	233.100,00	278.150,00	962.850,00
III.	SALE OF SERVICES	955.000,00	1.015.500,00	1.122.300,00	1.281.900,00	1.388.070,00	5.762.770,00
1.	Gym	480.000,00	522.000,00	599.000,00	684.500,00	753.650,00	3.039.150,00
2.	Individual work with a coach	475.000,00	493.500,00	523.300,00	597.400,00	634.420,00	2.723.620,00
IV.	OTHER INCOME						
	TOTAL INCOME (I+II+III+IV)	1.075.000,00	1.159.600,00	1.309.800,00	1.515.000,00	1.666.220,00	6.725.620,00

During the observed years of operation, total revenues from the sale of goods and services increase. The average sales of food products amount to 192,570.00, which amounts to a total of 962,850.00. The services are successfully performed and bring total revenues in the amount of 5,762,770.00. Total revenues are 6,725,620.00.

To make the most of revenue projections, they should be compared to projected expenses as seen in the table below.

PROJECT INCOME AND EXPENSE ITEMS		OBSERVED YEARS OF OPERATION					TOTAL
		Year 1	Year 2	Year 3	Year 4	Year 5	
I.	Total revenue	1.075.000,00	1.159.600,00	1.309.800,00	1.515.000,00	1.666.220,00	6.725.620,00
1.	Revenues from product placement						
2	Revenues from sales of goods	120.000,00	144.100,00	187.500,00	233.100,00	278.150,00	962.850,00
3.	Revenues from sales of services	955.000,00	1.015.500,00	1.122.300,00	1.281.900,00	1.388.070,00	5.762.770,00
4.	Other income						
II	Total expenses	1.136.400,00	1.087.600,00	966.060,00	884.880,00	879.300,00	4.954.240,00
1.	Material expenses	34.000,00	29.500,00	18.150,00	15.460,00	17.020,00	114.130,00
2.	Service costs	310.000,00	270.000,00	180.230,00	120.140,00	122.100,00	1.002.470,00
3.	Purchase time goods sold						
4.	Depreciation costs	73.000,00	73.000,00	73.000,00	73.000,00	68.990,00	360.990,00
5.	Staff costs - salaries	660.000,00	660.000,00	660.000,00	650.000,00	650.000,00	3.280.000,00
6.	Financial expenses	53.000,00	49.600,00	31.500,00	24.700,00	20.230,00	179.030,00
7.	Other expenses	6.400,00	5.500,00	3.180,00	1.580,00	960,00	17.620,00
III.	Total profit-loss (I-II)	-61.400,00	72.000,00	343.740,00	630.120,00	786.920,00	1.771.380,00
-	Income tax (20%)	-12.280,00	14.400,00	68.748,00	126.024,00	153.384,00	354.276,00
IV.	Net profit	-49.120,00	57.600,00	274.992,00	504.096,00	629.536,00	1.417.104,00
-	Legal reserves - 5%	-2.456,00	2.880,00	13.749,60	25.204,80	31.476,80	
-	Statutory reserves - 5%	-2.456,00	2.880,00	13.749,60	25.204,80	31.476,80	
-	Other reserves						
V.	Retained earnings	-44.208,00	51.840,00	247.492,80	453.686,40	566.582,40	1.275.393,60

The total revenues in 5 years of operation amounted to 6,725,620.00, expenses to 4,954,240.00. After deducting these items, the total profit is 1,771,380.00, after taxation of 20%, the net profit is 1,417,104.00. After the confiscation of reserves, the retained earnings in the cumulative amount after five years of operation amount to 1,275,393.60.

ITEMS OF RECEIPTS AND EXPENDITURES		OBSERVED YEARS OF OPERATION					TOTAL
		Year 1	Year 2	Year 3	Year 4	Year 5	
I.	TOTAL INCOME	0,00	1.075.000,00	1.159.600,00	1.309.800,00	1.515.000,00	2.334.220,00
1.	Total revenue		1.075.000,00	1.159.600,00	1.309.800,00	1.515.000,00	1.666.220,00
2.	The remaining value of fixed assets						
3.	The remaining value of working capital						668.000,00
II.	TOTAL EXPENDITURE	1.504.000,00	1.212.480,00	1.158.000,00	1.033.872,00	944.616,00	948.096,00
1.	Investments in fixed assets	836.000,00					
2.	Working capital investments	668.000,00					
3.	Expenses (excluding amor. And interest)		1.010.400,00	965.000,00	861.560,00	787.180,00	790.080,00
4.	Total tax. profit (20%)		202.080,00	193.000,00	172.312,00	157.436,00	158.016,00
III.	NET RECEIPTS (I.-II.)	-1.504.000,00	-137.480,00	1.600,00	275.928,00	570.384,00	1.386.124,00
IV.	NET CUMULATIVE RECEIPTS	-1.504.000,00	-1.641.480,00	-1.639.880,00	-1.363.952,00	-793.568,00	592.556,00

Total receipts increase during the observed period and amount to 7,393,620.00. The summarized tabular data of expenditures amount to 6,801,064.00. By subtracting the above, the calculation of net profit in the amount of 592,556.00 is obtained. A positive sign of net receipts occurs in the third year.

5 year Cash Flow

In order to be as reliable as possible, cash flow must be subject to accounting control, and to have the greatest possible expressive power, it must be subject to accounting analysis. A distinction needs to be made between submitted and accepted cash flow statements. The submitted estimates are the basis for decision-making within the planning or preparation of implementation and can offer several options to decide between, and the adopted estimates show the decision made by the company and are a criterion for comparison with achievements.

Cash flow planning allows a company to take timely action, which can be managing surpluses or providing the necessary cash. The cash flow planning process mustn't end with the preparation of a cash flow statement for a certain period, but this estimate is compared with the realized cash flow, identifies deviations from the plan, and corrects forward estimates.

The analysis of past, present and planned statements, i.e. balance sheet, income statement, and cash flow statement, as well as analysis of the business model and industry in which the company operates, must include calculations of various indicators, their size, and direction through years, which is the basis for any planning.

Cash flows are planned in the long term when the planned cash flow statements for several years are an integral part of strategic business plans, or in the short term when planning current solvency and preparing daily, weekly, monthly, quarterly, or annual cash flow estimates.

Usually, cash flow plans for longer periods (a year or more) are drawn up using the indirect method, which means that when planning cash flows from operations, operating revenues and operating expenses or operating profit are practically planned, which are adjusted for non-monetary items (depreciation, revaluation revenues, expenses) and all components of net current assets (receivables, inventories, and liabilities to suppliers).

The sales value plan is the starting point for cash flow planning, which reflects the wishes and expectations of the owners, management, and sales department, as well as the limitations represented by the available funds and financing possibilities. Based on the analysis of past years and the assessment of future possibilities, a long-term growth rate of sales revenue is planned, which is then the basis for planning all other business functions, starting with the production plan, followed by purchasing, human resources, and others.

The sales value plan is followed by the planning of other components of operating profit and components of net current assets. For simplicity, the most common methods for estimating these categories in practice are the percentage of sales method and the turnover coefficient method.

Long-term investment expenditure planning includes the planning of long-term investments, which can be investments in fixed assets, new long-term financial investments (acquisitions of competing companies), or investments in the market. Long-term investments are crucial for the company from a financial-strategic point of view, as they require long-term sources of financing, where capital plays a major role, so the owners must have the final say. When planning investments, the cooperation of the financial and production functions in the company is important, as they determine the method and volume of production in the future. The aim of planning this expenditure is to anticipate the most favorable moment when the implementation of the plan will require as little external borrowing as possible. Investments increase fixed costs, financial expenses, and also have a positive effect on the efficiency of assets, which directly affects the increase in profit margin.

Companies invest in strategic investments (new program, new market, new technology), which must bring positive cash flow, and in support or complementary investments (for example, warehousing), which support strategic investments and do not necessarily bring positive cash flow. Decisions on long-term investments are among the most important business decisions for the company, as they significantly determine the conditions of business in the future and have long-term positive, but also negative consequences for the development of the company. Even one major failed investment that does not bring the planned cash flow can greatly worsen a company's financial position in the future or even bankruptcy. Therefore, even before the decision on the investment is made, the companies manage the process called the investment program, and the already started investment is carefully monitored by comparing the effects of the investment with the planned ones and taking appropriate action on that basis.

In the fourth step of preparation of investment programs, several methods are used for the analysis and evaluation of investment projects, and according to the criterion of including the time dimension, they are divided into so-called static and dynamic evaluation methods. Static methods, which include mainly the payback period, the discounted payback period, and the accounting rate of return, do not include the time component or take it into account only partially or indirectly. Dynamic methods, which include net present value, internal rate of return, revised internal rate of return, and profitability index, by discounting future cash flows allow the time-varying effects of the investment to be comparable, to compare their present values. Due to the inclusion of the time component of cash flows, dynamic methods are more suitable for deciding on the adequacy of an investment. The most appropriate methods (from most appropriate to least appropriate) for deciding on the suitability or unsuitability of investments are: net present value, adjusted internal rate of return, internal rate of return, profitability index, normal payback period, discounted payback period, and to a lesser extent accounting return.

Long-term planning of cash flows in financing begins with the planning of expenses, which includes planning the return of long-term financial liabilities and interest in accordance with payment plans, planning the distribution of profits to owners, and planning possible purchases of own shares or stakes. When we add planned expenditures or receipts in financing to the planned cash flow from operations and investments, only precisely planned expenditures are equal to planned receipts, we usually have a surplus of receipts or a surplus of expenditures. With surplus receipts, we can increase planned financing expenses (higher dividends, repurchases of treasury shares, early repayment of loans), and increase expenditures on short-term or long-term investments. The surplus of expenditure over receipts arising from an increase in long-term assets (new long-term investments) or an increase in automatic net current assets having the character of long-term assets is generally covered by receipts from new long-term sources such as equity and long-term loans. The surplus of expenditures over receipts, which arises from the increase in short-term funds, is financed from short-term financial sources.

To show cash flow projection we are going to use the same example as above.

ITEMS OF RECEIPTS AND EXPENDITURES		OBSERVED YEARS OF OPERATION					TOTAL
		Year 1	Year 2	Year 3	Year 4	Year 5	
I	TOTAL INCOME	1.504.000,00	1.075.000,00	1.159.600,00	1.309.800,00	1.515.000,00	2.334.220,00
1.	Total revenue		1.075.000,00	1.159.600,00	1.309.800,00	1.515.000,00	1.666.220,00
2.	Own sources of funding	1.104.000,00					
3.	Share capital						
4.	Bank loans	400.000,00					
5.	Commodity loans						
6.	The remaining value of fixed assets						
7.	The remaining value of working capital						668.000,00
8.	Reserve requirements						
9.	Optional reserves						
II	TOTAL EXPENDITURE	1.504.000,00	1.331.491,41	1.272.144,80	1.141.969,39	1.047.287,17	1.046.866,56
1.	Investments in fixed assets	836.000,00					
2.	Working capital investments	668.000,00					
3.	Expenses (excluding depreciation and interest)		1.010.400,00	965.000,00	861.560,00	787.190,00	790.080,00
4.	Income tax (20%)		202.080,00	193.000,00	172.312,00	157.436,00	158.016,00
5.	Reserve requirements		10.104,00	9.650,00	8.615,60	7.871,80	7.900,80
6.	Optional reserves		10.104,00	9.650,00	8.615,60	7.871,80	7.900,80
7.	Bank loan annuities		98.803,41	94.844,80	90.886,19	86.927,57	82.968,96
8.	Commodity loan annuities						
9.	Dividends (possibly)						
III	NET RECEIPTS (I.-II.)	0	-256.491,41	-112.544,80	167.810,61	467.712,83	1.287.353,44
IV.	NET CUMULATIVE RECEIPTS	0	-256.491,41	-369.036,21	-201.225,60	266.487,23	1.553.840,67

In the stated projection of cash flows, the total receipts are in the amount of 8,897,620.00, and the expenditures are 7,343,779.33, and by subtraction, a net receipt in the amount of 1,553,840.67 is obtained.

Sensitivity analysis consists of the procedures of analyzing the project with various negative situations that may occur during its lifetime. Starting from the above definition, and the possible different factors that this entrepreneurial venture could face during its operational period, in the sensitivity analysis, the project (for all five years) was tested with 4 risk assumptions:

- First assumption: a reduction of total revenues for 10%

- Second assumption: an increase in total salary by 5%

- Third assumption: an increase in material costs by 10%

- Fourth assumption: an increase in material costs by 5%

ITEMS OF RECEIPTS AND EXPENDITURES		OBSERVED YEARS OF OPERATION					TOTAL
		Year 1	Year 2	Year 3	Year 4	Year 5	
IA	Total income A	1.075.000,00	1.159.600,00	1.309.800,00	1.515.000,00	1.666.220,00	6.725.620,00
-	(less) First assumption (-10%)	107.500,00	115.960,00	130.980,00	151.500,00	166.622,00	672.562,00
-	(less) Second assumption (-5%)	53.750,00	57.980,00	65.490,00	75.750,00	83.311,00	336.281,00
I. B	Total income B	913.750,00	985.660,00	1.113.330,00	1.287.750,00	1.416.287,00	5.716.777,00
II. A	Total expenses A	1.136.400,00	1.087.600,00	966.060,00	894.890,00	879.300,00	4.964.240,00
-	(more) Third assumption (10%)	113.640,00	108.760,00	96.606,00	89.489,00	87.930,00	496.424,00
-	(more) Fourth assumption (5%)	56.820,00	54.380,00	48.303,00	44.744,00	43.965,00	248.212,00
II. B	Total expenses B	1.306.860,00	1.250.740,00	1.110.969,00	1.029.112,00	1.011.195,00	5.708.876,00
III A	TOTAL PROFIT A (IA-IIA)	-61.400,00	72.000,00	343.740,00	620.120,00	786.920,00	1.761.380,00
III B	TOTAL PROFIT B (IB-IIB)	-393.110,00	-265.080,00	2.361,00	258.638,00	405.092,00	7.901,00
P1	(less) 20% income tax A		14.400,00	68.748,00	124.024,00	157.384,00	364.556,00
P2	(less) 20% income tax B			472,20	51.727,60	81.018,40	133.218,20
IV A	NET PROFIT A (IIIA-P1)		57.600,00	274.992,00	496.096,00	629.536,00	1.458.224,00
IV B	NET PROFIT B (IIIB-P2)			1.888,80	206.910,40	324.073,60	532.872,80

The table shows how the net profit after loading gets a positive sign in the 3rd year of project operation. This is proof of the success of this entrepreneurial venture.

CRITICAL METRICS TO ANALYZE STABILITY

Profitable performance and financial security are prerequisites for successful business operations in a dynamic market environment. The success of the company, with the present uncertainty and risks, is observed through the ability and skills of management to provide and preserve the current ability to pay and create good conditions for a long-term profitable business. Given the present financial and business risks, the management has the task to, through the structure of assets and the manner of its financing, contribute to strengthening long-term security and creating a stable basis for future business.

The company's ability to service operating and financial liabilities is a key indicator of good financial condition. The financial health of the company is the basic concern of creditors, but also of investors who can settle their receivables from the company only if there are sufficient funds to service the company's debt. The financial statements individually cannot provide complete information on the ability to meet due to short-term liabilities. The balance sheet provides information useful for assessing the financial balance and efficiency of an enterprise's assets and capital management. The amount of required and available funds is determined based on information from the cash flow statement. Coverage indicators are an important tool for analyzing the financial security of companies, as they can monitor the relationship between the accounting categories contained in the various financial statements.

Cash Flow to Long Term Debt Ratio (How long it will take to pay off long term debt with cash flow)

While it is unreasonable for an organization to commit the entirety of its income to debt reimbursement, the cash flow to debt ratio gives a concise review of the organization's general finance related status. A high ratio indicates that the company is better able to repay its debt and is, therefore, able to take on more debt if needed.

Another way to calculate the cash flow to debt ratio is to observe a company's EBITDA rather than operating cash flow. This option is used less frequently because it involves investing in inventories, and since the inventory may not sell quickly, it is not considered liquid as cash from operations.

Some analysts use free cash flow instead of cash flow from operations because this measure takes away money used for capital expenditures. Using free cash flow instead of operating cash flow may therefore indicate that the company is less able to meet its obligations.

The cash flow to debt ratio examines the amount of cash flow compared to total debt. Analysts sometimes also examine the ratio of cash flow to long-term debt alone. This ratio can provide a more favorable picture of a company's financial health if it has assumed significant short-term debt. When examining any of these ratios, it is important to remember that they differ greatly in different industries. This means, for the indicators to be understood and analyzed properly, they should be contracted to the ratios of rival companies in the same or similar industry.

Example:

The total financial debt is 60.000 and cash equivalents are 2.000. Accordingly, the net debt amounts to 58.000. Assuming that EBITDA is 25.000 then Net Debt / EBITDA is 2.32 which is relatively low indebtedness. The upper limit of indebtedness is 5x, which means that the company is capable of additional borrowing.

Debt to Asset Ratio

The debt-to-assets ratio measures the total assets financed by creditors instead of investors. In other words, it shows what percentage of funds are financed by borrowing compared to the percentage of funds financed by investors.

It illustrates how the company has grown and acquired its assets over time. Companies can generate investor interest in obtaining capital, make a profit to acquire their own assets, or take on debt. The first two are desirable in most cases.

This is an important measurement because it shows how much of a company's assets are owned by shareholders in the form of shares, and how many resources are owned by creditors in the form of debt. This value is used by both financial specialists and banks to settle on choices about the organization.

Financial specialists need to ensure the organization is solvent, has enough money to meet its present commitments, and is successful enough to pay a rate of profitability. On the other hand, creditors want to see how much debt the company already has because it concerns collateral and the possibility of repayment. If the company has already used up all of its assets and is barely meeting its monthly payments, the lender is unlikely to extend any additional credit.

Analysts, investors, and creditors use this measure to assess a company's overall risk. Companies with a higher value are considered riskier to invest and lend because they are more indebted. This means that companies with higher metering will have to pay a higher percentage of their profits in principle and pay interest than companies of the same size with a lower ratio. So lower is always better.

The key thing to remember is that if 100% of your asset base is financed by debt, you are bankrupt! You want to keep your debt to asset ratio in line with your business. You also want to look at the historical patterns in your business and your ability to cover interest expenses on debt.

Example:

On the balance sheet for 2018, the total assets are 3,373. To get total debt, you need to add together current debt (short-term liabilities), which is 543, and long-term debt, which is 531. The calculation becomes:

Property Debt = (543 + 531) / 3373 = 31.84%

The debt-to-asset ratio for the corporation is 31.84%, meaning that 31.84% of the company's assets are purchased with debt. As a result, 68.16% of the company's assets are financed with capital or investors.

We don't know if this is good or bad because we don't have industry data to compare. We can, for example, look at the ratio for 2017. The value is 27.79%. From 2017 to 2088, the debt-to-assets ratio decreased from 31.84% to 27.79%.

A drop in the debt-to-assets ratio may be a good thing, but we need more information to analyze it appropriately.

TIME VALUE OF MONEY

Inflation is one of the most important economic concepts. It represents a general increase in the prices of products and services within an economic area (the phenomenon of price growth). Inflation is actually the rate at which prices of products and services have increased over a period. Due to such a phenomenon, the purchasing power of the population in the country is decreasing over time.

Precisely because of inflation, money is considered to have a time value. This simply means that due to rising prices, the value of money decreases over time. Namely, with inflation, an individual can no longer buy the same amount of products and services with the same amount of money as they could a year ago. E.g. if the annual inflation rate is 5%, it means that a product that cost 100 a year ago now costs 105 (price + inflation). So, with inflation, the value of every monetary unit is lower.

Inflation is usually measured with the consumer price index (CPI) but also with some other statistical indices. The basket that represents the index contains products and services such as food, clothing, fuel, computers, hairdressing services, and the like. The level of inflation is determined in relation to the change in the value of the basket of products and services in a given timeframe. If at the end of the year the total value of the basket is 10% more expensive, then we are talking about an annual inflation rate of 10%.

There are various causes for inflation. One of the more important is the excessive increase in the money supply. When a larger amount of money follows a smaller amount of products and services, an imbalance of the commodity-money relationship occurs, which leads to a logical increase in prices and a decrease in the value of money.

The role of the supervisor and controller of inflation in the country is usually played by the central bank, which with its monetary policy tries to keep the inflation rate stable (2-3%). Because of its correlation with the unemployment rate, moderate inflation is desirable.

With this in mind, it is important to state that money, i.e. capital, is not free, i.e. that it has its price. For some sources of financing (bonds), this price represents the real cost of financing for the company and thus reflects the actual issuance of cash based on interest. On the other hand, with certain internal sources of self-financing (accumulated profit, depreciation) there is no actual issuance of cash, but this price is defined as a "calculative price", which is an opportunity cost. The prices of individual sources of financing depend on the market and the relationship between supply and demand, but not only on that, which can best be seen from the structure of interest rates. Interest rates are the basic prices of debt financial instruments that affect the movements of all segments of financial markets, and therefore macroeconomic developments in the economy. They also affect the making of business, especially the strategic decisions of individual companies, as well as our private lives. In the following, a complete distinction should be made between the concepts of interest rate and interest. Namely, the interest rate represents the annual rate of return on the investment and the financial instrument until its maturity, while interest should mean the monetary equivalent of the interest rate expressed in units of a particular currency. Thus, it is reasonable to argue that the interest rate is the price of money.

Simple interest is an interest that is paid (calculated) only on the original amount or borrowed principal. Simple interest is not used in business practice to calculate value over time. Compound interest is used instead. Compound interest implies that the interest paid (earned) on the loan is periodically added to the principal. As a result, interest is accrued on both interest and initial principal.

Calculating the present value of future cash flows allows us to place all cash flows at the current level so that we can compare them within the limits of today's value of money. The process of calculating the present value of future cash flows is also called discounting, and the interest rate used is the discount interest rate. Therefore, the discount interest rate is the one by which we convert the future values of cash flows into the present value.

If e.g. we invest 100 for a period of three years with an interest rate of 5% per year, which means that the initial investment at the end of the first year increased to 105 (stake of 100 increased by 5% interest). When you go to the end of the second year, the value of 105 from the end of the first year increases to 110.25, because during the second year you

102

received 5% interest on the initial deposit of 100, and 0.25 interest per 5 units that were the interest accrued to the principal at the end of the first year. When the interest rate of 5% per annum is applied to the calculation base from the beginning of the third year of 110.25, the total amount of 115.76 is obtained at the end of the third year, which represents the future value for 100 for a period of 3 years with an annual interest rate of 5%. The calculation of the future value, in this case, is synthesized in the following table:

Year	Basis for calculation	Interest rate (r)	Interest rate factor (1 + r)	Interest amount	Amount at the end of the period
n	1	2	3	4=(1*3)	1+4
1	100	5%	1,05	5	105
2	105	5%	1,05	5,25	110,25
3	110,25	5%	1,05	5,51	115,76
			Total	15,76	

By summarizing the data from the presented example, it is clear that the future value of the present investment (FV) for any maturity and interest is calculated by the formula

$$FV = PV (1 + r)^n$$

The presented analysis of future value is based on the assumption that interest is paid annually, although it is not uncommon for interest to be calculated and attributed to equity at shorter intervals. The general

formula for calculating the future value of deposits at the end of the year

n when interest is paid **m** times a year is

$$FV = PV (1 + r/m)^{nm}$$

Below we see how the value of 1 monetary unit changes during the years,

depending on the value of the interest rate.

n	0%	1%	2%	3%	4%	5%	6%	7%	8%
0	1,0000	1,0000	1,0000	1,0000	1,0000	1,0000	1,0000	1,0000	1,0000
5	1,0000	1,0510	1,1041	1,1593	1,2167	1,2763	1,3382	1,4026	1,4693
10	1,0000	1,1046	1,2190	1,3439	1,4802	1,6289	1,7908	1,9672	2,1589
15	1,0000	1,1610	1,3459	1,5580	1,8009	2,0789	2,3966	2,7590	3,1722
20	1,0000	1,2202	1,4859	1,8061	2,1911	2,6533	3,2071	3,8697	4,6610
25	1,0000	1,2824	1,6406	2,0938	2,6658	3,3864	4,2919	5,4274	6,8485

The calculation methodology presented is very simple when it

comes to only one or a few amounts to be accumulated. The matter is

more complicated if there are many such amounts when computer

programs for spreadsheets are of great help.

COST OF CAPITAL AND RISK MANAGEMENT

Although the term cost of capital often includes the financial costs of all sources of financing of an investment project, in a narrower sense it is exclusively the required rate of return on invested funds. There are different components of corporate financing where investors or creditors demand compensation in the form of dividend or interest yield: the cost of share capital, the cost of debt, and the cost of preferred shares. Apart from the nature of the financial instrument, the maturity of the financing cost, the risk, and the priority of the payment, the cost of capital is a first-class issue of investment activities. Capital is the long-term and riskiest form of corporate financing.

Business practice most often argues that the cost of capital will increase with a negative impact on the exposure of banks to risky business activities. Risks are not easy to anticipate or manage, which is why banks strive to have as much capital and reserves as possible in the event of the need to cover unexpected losses.

Cost of Capital

Financing, as one of the key functions of every company, implies an agreed form of compensation to the owners of capital, which represents the cost of capital. The mentioned cost of capital, in simple terms, is defined as the required rate of return on various forms of financing.

There are three basic approaches to determining the cost of share capital:

1. Dividend cost approach

The belief that equity has no cost if dividends were paid has long been refuted. An equity investor will always have an opportunity cost, expressed through earnings that would be achievable through investing in other businesses of similar risk.

When buying shares, investors expect cash flow through dividends paid during the holding of shares, and from the expected proft when selling shares. With this approach, the cost of share capital can be shown as the present value of dividends to infinity as the expected sale price of the share is determined by future dividends.

The cost approach from the aspect of dividends, although simple, applies only to companies that pay dividends.

Also, it is unrealistic to expect rates to continue to rise at the same rate. Many societies are growing at unequal and unpredictable rates. Therefore, to calculate the cost of capital by valuing dividends that do not have constant growth, a multi-stage discounting model is applied.

There are cases where the dividend does not increase. In this scenario, the company is expected to pay all its profits to shareholders. The cost of a zero-growth share (i.e., the required shareholder rate of return) that yields a continuous constant dividend is calculated by dividing the perpetual dividend by the current market price of the share.

2. Cost approach from risk aspect

Risk and expected return are closely related. If we talk about the risk-free rate, it is equal to the sum of the actual rate of return and the inflation premium. When investing or taking on potential risk, the risk premium is a reward for making risky investments.

Investment risk

When investing in individual securities, there are two types of risk: (1) Non-systemic risk or diversifying risk and (2) Systemic risk or unavoidable risk. It follows that total risk is the sum of systemic and unsystemic risk.

Unsystemic risk

Unsystematic risk is caused by the company/issuer of securities. This risk is eliminated through diversification, i.e. through investing in multiple securities. Accordingly, investors do not even expect a premium for exposure to unsystematic risk as it can be eliminated.

Keep in mind the importance of diversification. Namely, unsystemic risk, i.e. risk that can be reduced by diversification, accounts for more than 50% of the total risk of a particular security, which is a very obvious reason for portfolio diversification.

Systemic risk

Systemic risk is the general risk of the market arising from changes in the world or national economy, tax reform, and the political situation.

Market factors that are part of the systemic i.e. of unavoidable risk cannot be diversified. Therefore a certain premium is expected on them.

- Beta

The measure of the systemic risk of a particular security is expressed through beta. It is a measure that shows the volatility of a security relative to the market. If there are a set of different securities in the portfolio, then the total beta of the portfolio is the weighted average beta of the individual securities. If the beta is greater than 1, we are talking about an aggressive investment, that is, that the security has a higher risk than the systemic risk. If the beta is less than 1, the security risk is lower than the systemic risk.

- The Capital Asset Pricing Model (CAPM)

This is a model that analyzes the relationship between portfolio risk and return on capital. Using this model, we obtain a strong analytical basis for determining the relationship between risk and return.

Concerning the previously mentioned model of continuous dividend growth, the CAPM model can be applied to all companies regardless of the (in) stability of their growth, and regardless of whether they pay dividends or not.

The disadvantage of the CAPM model is that the market risk premium and beta, as factors in the calculation, are based on historical data. Also, it is much more complicated to calculate the cost of invested capital using the CAPM model.

3. Cost approach from the cost of debt before tax plus a risk premium

The cost of share capital is the required return on risk-free investment increased by the market portfolio risk premium multiplied by the beta. As with the above approach, diversification does not reduce market risk, and risk-free investment is considered to be investing in government bonds.

In this approach, the cost of pre-tax debt forms the basis for estimating the cost of a company's equity, as analysts often estimate the cost of equity by adding a certain risk premium to the cost of a company's pre-tax debt. Accordingly, the required rate of return on investors is higher for a company that has a higher borrowing cost.

According to this method, every company should have an interest in establishing an ideal capital structure, i.e. a combination of stock, debt, and retained earnings that allow for a maximum stock price.

The cost of capital is a necessary economic and accounting tool that calculates investment opportunity costs and maximizes the profitability of potential investments.

It is extremely important to correctly apply certain methods of calculating the cost of capital, since each component of the capital contains its own, individual cost expressed through the discount rate.

Weighted Average Cost of Capital

WACC or a weighted average cost of capital is a financial ratio that calculates the cost of financing and acquiring a company's assets by comparing the company's debt and ownership structure. In other words, this indicator measures the severity of debt and the actual cost of borrowing money or raising funds through the capital to finance new capital investments and expansions based on the current level of debt and the ownership structure of the company. Management typically uses this ratio to decide whether a company should use debt or equity to finance new investments.

This ratio is very extensive because it includes all sources of capital; including long-term debt, ordinary shares, preference shares, and bonds to measure the average borrowing price. It is also extremely complex. Determining the price of debt is straightforward. Bonds and long-term debt are issued with stated interest rates that can be used to calculate their total price. On the other hand, share capital, as well as ordinary and preferred shares, does not have a visible and definite price. Instead, we need to calculate the price before applying it to the equation.

Therefore, many investors and creditors do not focus on this measurement as the only indicator of the cost of capital. The estimate of the cost of capital is based on several different assumptions that may vary from investor to investor.

Here is an example of how to calculate WACC.

Some time ago, a company issued 350.000 bonds with a nominal value of 100. The market price of these bonds today is 85,72. Besides, the company owns preferred shares with an accounting value of 15.000.000 and a market value of 10.000.000. In the capital structure of this company, we can also find common stock, 1.000.000 pieces with a nominal value of 50. The market value of common shares is 70. We need to calculate the weighted average cost of capital, if the rate of return required by common shareholders is 12%, owners of preferred shares 80%, and owners of bonds and 5,5%. When calculating, we will ignore the savings made based on tax deductions. The capital structure of the company can be shown in the following table:

Sources of funding	Accounting value	Market value	The price of capital
	In 000	In 000	%
Bonds	35.000	30.000	5.5
Preference shares	15.000	10.000	8
Ordinary shares	50.000	70.000	12
TOTAL:	100.000	110.000	

We obtained the book value of the bonds by multiplying the total number of issued bonds by the nominal value of 350.000 * 100= 35.000.000, and we obtained the market value of the bonds by the number of issued bonds and the market price of these bonds 350.000 * 85,72 = 30.000.000. In the same way, the market value of the common shares of the company was obtained.

When calculating the cost of capital, we start from the market value of individual sources of financing and determine their share in total capital, so we have:

$$w_s = \frac{E}{V} = \frac{70.000.000}{110.000.000} = 0.64$$

$$w_{ps} = \frac{P}{V} = \frac{10.000.000}{110.000.000} = 0.09$$

$$w_d = \frac{D}{V} = \frac{30.000.000}{110.000.000} = 0.27$$

The share of capital obtained by issuing bonds in the total capital of the company is 27%. The share of capital obtained by issuing ordinary shares in the total capital of the company is 64%, and the share of capital obtained by issuing preferred shares is 9%.

We can now calculate the weighted average cost of capital:

$$WACC = w_s r_s + w_{ps} r_{ps} + w_d r_d =$$
$$= 0.64 * 12\% + 0.09 * 8\% + 0.27 * 5.5\% =$$
$$= 7.64\% + 0.73\% + 1.5\% = 9.86\%$$

The company must know its weighted average cost of capital as a way of measuring financing costs for future projects. The lower the weighted average cost of capital of a company, the cheaper it will be to finance new projects. The weighted average cost of capital is the total return required by the company. This is why company directors often use a weighted average cost of capital to make decisions. In this way, they can determine the economic feasibility of the merger and other expansive possibilities.

The weighted average cost of capital in the example above is 9.86%. This means that for every $1 that the company receives from investors, it must pay them almost $0.10 in return.

In other words, this is the minimum acceptable rate of return that the firm should earn on its investments of average risk, to be profitable.

A company looking to reduce its WACC may decide to increase the use of cheaper sources of funding. For example, the company in the example may issue more bonds instead of shares because it may receive cheaper financing. Because this would increase the share of debt to equity and because debt is cheaper than equity, the weighted average cost of capital of a company will decrease.

Risk Management

The risk management process consists of four phases: risk identification, risk measurement, decision making, and communication (risk treatment).

Risk identification has a significant impact on the quality of the risk management process, as all other steps take part afterwards. The risk management process begins with creating a list of all the risks to which the company is exposed. The identified risks are most often the result of a previous analysis of the company's environment. Following the widespread diversification of the environment into layers of general, competitive, and internal environment, it can be said that subject of analysis are the risks of the general environment, industry risks, and company risks. This division is useful from the aspect of techniques used in the analysis of the environment, and for the needs of risk management in the company.

After identifying the risks that come from all layers of the environment, it is useful to classify them into precisely defined categories. Regardless of the activity, all companies are characterized by the existence of financial, operational, and strategic risks, so such a division makes the most sense.

The measurement phase is the cornerstone of an effective risk management process in a company. When risk measurement is done systematically and consistently throughout the company, management is in a position to make decisions that respect risk information. An adequate risk measurement system provides the company with an unambiguous insight into the level of exposure to risk factors, individually and collectively. In this way, management's attention is focused on priority risks.

The primary objective of risk measurement is to determine risk exposure. Determining risk exposure has its final expression in a numerical indicator that can refer to the total risk exposure or the expected impact of risk on the company's results under appropriate assumptions.

Decisions are made based on the results of risk measurement models. The sophistication of the models vary depending on the activity, reaching the highest degree of complexity in financial services and energy trade. Measuring risk without making decisions that can change the natural course of events in the future is just a waste of limited resources (time, effort, and talent). The risk decision-making phase has two important outputs: defining risk appetites and appropriate limits, and making specific decisions about eliminating, transferring, sharing, and taking a risk.

STATISTICAL METHODS TO ANALYZE IMPACTS OF CHANGES

Changes and phenomena in a company's environment affect its behavior, which is why management feels the need to monitor, record, consider, and explain these changes and phenomena. With the development of human society, the way of observing and presenting these phenomena changed, so methods for their description were developed.

Statistical analysis involves the manipulation of quantitative and qualitative data to describe phenomena and to draw conclusions about the relationships between variables.

ANOVA method to analyze statistical significance

As the name suggests, variance analysis deals with the variances between standard and actual values. Analysis of variance compares the actual with the predicted values and indicates areas where things are not going according to plan.

Analysis of variances is a comparison of realized and planned quantities.

For example, the company achieved sales of 95, and sales of 100 were planned. There is a negative variance of -5 or -5%. Or the maintenance sector incurred costs of 45.000 and planned 50.000. There is a positive variance of +5.000 EUR or + 10%.

The most common variations observed are the ratio of achieved and planned, achieved, and last year's results, as well as projected and planned results.

Analysis of variance is a tool by which financial controllers and financial managers of companies interpret deviations of the business result in relation to the result predicted by the budget or budget revision during the year.

It also serves the company's management to see all aspects of the business, to react on time to potential problems, and to work with its associates to eliminate those problems, all to maximize results and increase the company's productivity.

Analysis of variances is done in companies every month during the "closing" of the period and thus allows the company's management to see in time all the anomalies in the company, to prepare action plans for the coming period to correct deviations (in this case we mean negative deviations because positive deviations mean improved results) and thus avoid possible negative effects on the company's result.

The analysis of variances starts from the company's budget and the current result is explained through different variances. As already mentioned, the month, period, and the whole business year can be compared, with the fact that the analysis of variances at the end of the year cannot serve as a tool for correction, but only as a final explanation of deviations from the planned result.

Analysis of variance can be presented using a table and graphs depending on which level of detail you want to see and at which level the current result is considered.

T-test method to analyze change in mean

The T-test is a method to analyze two different sets of data and analyze if their difference is significant. For example, you may see one branch of your company's sales in Europe performing better than the one in America. On doing a t-test, you may realize that the increase (difference in sales) is insignificant, and it is only due to the variances in both data sets.

Examples of each

ANOVA

The budget represents the company's plan for the next period and as such must be compiled with maximum care and taking into account all aspects that may affect the business result.

The sales plan and sales mix developed by the sales sector are usually taken as the basis for budgeting. Based on the sales plan, other parts of the company create parts of the budget from their share of responsibility.

Sale	Jan	Feb	Mar	Apr	May	Jun	Jul	Aug	Sept	Oct	Nov	Dec	Yearly
Product A	124.003	115.737	128.137	234.063	255.985	247.728	255.985	249.902	247.728	255.985	247.728	247.728	2.610.708
Product B	26.015	23.697	27.324	26.332	26.682	18.391	17.929	21.359	19.171	21.662	26.913	27.235	282.710
In total	150.018	139.434	155.460	260.395	282.668	266.119	273.915	271.261	266.898	277.647	274.641	274.963	2.893.419

When we talk about material costs, based on the components of the product, the amount of material needed for production is calculated, which is in accordance with the requirements of sales. An important aspect of material costs is the price of materials, and this is where the Procurement Department / Sector enters the scene, giving its forecast of the price of direct materials. It usually ranges from current prices and based on them an assessment is given in terms of, the efficiency of Procurement through better negotiation aspects, to the movement of raw materials on the world market.

In this way, we come to the cost plan of direct material. In the table below a table of consumption of direct material in kg and also prices of direct material has been made. For simplicity, in this example, we consider the total material required to produce two finished products.

Basic material Ton.	Jan	Feb	Mar	Apr	May	Jun	Jul	Aug	Sept	Oct	Nov	Dec	Yearly
Product A	6.473	6.041	6.689	12.218	13.362	12.931	13.362	13.045	12.931	13.362	12.931	12.931	136.279
Product B	2.565	2.337	2.694	2.596	2.631	1.813	1.768	2.106	1.890	2.136	2.654	2.685	27.875
In total	9.038	8.378	9.383	14.814	15.993	14.745	15.130	15.151	14.822	15.498	15.585	15.617	164.154

Basic material Mon.unit	Jan	Feb	Mar	Apr	May	Jun	Jul	Aug	Sept	Oct	Nov	Dec	Yearly
Product A	58	58	58	58	58	58	58	58	58	58	58	58	58
Product B	58	58	58	58	58	58	58	58	58	58	58	58	58

To be able to calculate the required number of direct workers needed to meet the planned level of production, we need the time to make the product. The table below shows the number of direct hours based on the production time per unit of product. The production time for product A is 0.18 hours and for product B 0.19 hours.

Product A	Jan	Feb	Mar	Apr	May	Jun	Jul	Aug	Sept	Oct	Nov	Dec	Yearly
Amount	124.003	115.737	128.137	234.063	255.985	247.728	255.985	249.902	247.728	255.985	247.728	247.728	2.610.708
Hours of making	0,18	0,18	0,18	0,18	0,18	0,18	0,18	0,18	0,18	0,18	0,18	0,18	0,18
Number of hours	22.321	20.833	23.065	42.131	46.077	44.591	46.077	44.982	44.591	46.077	44.591	44.591	469.927

Product B	Jan	Feb	Mar	Apr	May	Jun	Jul	Aug	Sept	Oct	Nov	Dec	Yearly
Amount	26.015	23.697	27.324	26.332	26.682	18.391	17.929	21.359	19.171	21.662	26.913	27.235	282.710
Hours of making	0,19	0,19	0,19	0,19	0,19	0,19	0,19	0,19	0,19	0,19	0,19	0,19	0,19
Number of hours	5.060	4.609	5.314	5.122	5.190	3.577	3.487	4.154	3.729	4.213	5.235	5.297	54.987

Based on the calculated number of hours, the work planning service calculates the required number of direct workers, but also the required number of indirect workers related to production. These are mainly workers who are not directly involved in the production process, such as maintenance or quality control workers. The number of administrative workers is fixed and mostly unchanged, starting from the current situation, taking into account the need for new employment or an optimization plan that would include the reduction or elimination of certain jobs. Administrative workers in production are the leaders of plants, shifts, departments. All this is taken into account including the number of working days required for a given level of production.

	Jan	Feb	Mar	Apr	May	Jun	Jul	Aug	Sept	Oct	Nov	Dec	Yearly
Theoretical days	22	20	22	22	21	22	23	21	22	22	21	23	261
Work days	19	18	22	20	20	22	23	11	22	22	20	13	232
Number of direct workers	252	252	251	252	252	251	251	251	251	251	252	251	251
Number of indirect workers	76	76	75	75	75	75	75	75	75	75	75	75	75
Number of adm. workers	25	25	25	25	25	25	25	25	25	25	25	25	25

After defining the required number of employees by the work planning service, the Human Resources Department together with the Company's Management harmonizes the salary policy. The process starts from the current level of salaries and on that basis possible planned corrections for the next year, taking into account the cost of living, the average salary in the Republic, Region, Municipality. The salaries of new employees are also taken into consideration.

Along with the estimation of earnings, in the production part of the company, the costs of transformation are calculated. The level of internal scrap, the need for indirect material and maintenance material, as well as the level of costs of production services are assessed.

The technical service, based on the level of production, calculates the amount of electricity, gas, and industrial water and gives an estimate of energy prices and its movement in the future, based on current prices in cooperation with the Procurement sector.

When everyone has finished their estimates and calculations, they send the data to the Controlling / Finance Department of the company, which is responsible for systematization, and preparation and control of the budget and budgeting process. The controlling department calculates the depreciation costs, based on the useful life of existing fixed assets and the depreciation rate for each individual asset, as well as on the basis of an estimate of future investments in the depreciation product for future activated fixed assets.

The data collected in this way is the basis needed to calculate the cost price of our products.

Mon. units	Jan	Feb	Mar	Apr	May	Jun
Production volume	150.018	139.434	155.460	260.395	282.668	266.119
Direct hours	27.380	25.442	28.379	47.253	51.267	48.168
Basic material						
Product A	7.192.200	6.712.720	7.431.940	13.575.660	14.847.140	14.368.200
Product B	1.495.846	1.362.581	1.571.103	1.514.110	1.534.235	1.057.493
Total	8.688.046	8.075.301	9.003.043	15.089.770	16.381.375	15.425.693
Direct work	21.356.775	19.844.493	22.135.673	36.857.341	39.988.298	37.571.078
Indirect work	1.100.385	1.061.775	1.293.435	1.177.605	1.177.605	1.293.435
Administration	1.511.248	1.512.500	1.507.500	1.509.750	1.509.750	1.507.500
Packaging material	3.315.401	3.081.483	3.435.675	5.754.740	6.246.952	5.881.225
Services	10.300.000	10.300.000	10.300.000	10.300.000	10.300.000	10.300.000
Energy	35.704.321	33.185.199	36.999.581	61.974.119	67.274.871	63.336.266
Other costs	2.575.000	2.575.000	2.575.000	2.575.000	2.575.000	2.575.000
Load costs	54.506.355	51.715.957	56.111.192	83.291.213	89.084.178	84.893.425
Transformation costs	75.863.130	71.560.450	78.246.865	120.148.554	129.072.476	122.464.504
Amortization	14.111.667	14.111.667	14.111.667	14.111.667	14.111.667	14.111.667
Transformation costs	89.974.797	85.672.116	92.358.531	134.260.221	143.184.143	136.576.170
Product costs	98.662.842	93.747.417	101.361.574	149.349.991	159.565.518	152.001.863

Mon. units	Jul	Aug	Sept	Oct	Nov	Dec	Yearly
Production volume	273.915	271.261	266.898	277.647	274.641	274.963	2.893.419
Direct hours	49.565	49.137	48.320	50.291	49.826	49.888	524.915
Basic material							
Product A	14.847.140	14.494.340	14.368.200	14.847.140	14.368.200	14.368.200	151.421.080
Product B	1.030.941	1.228.132	1.102.309	1.245.551	1.547.511	1.566.029	16.255.842
Total	15.878.081	15.722.472	15.470.509	16.092.691	15.915.711	15.934.229	167.676.922
Direct work	38.660.389	38.326.646	37.689.323	39.226.625	38.863.960	38.912.820	409.433.421
Indirect work	1.351.350	646.718	1.293.435	1.293.435	1.177.605	762.548	13.629.330
Administration	1.506.522	1.507.500	1.507.500	1.507.500	1.509.750	1.504.038	18.101.058
Packaging material	6.053.512	5.994.873	5.898.450	6.135.997	6.069.562	6.076.680	63.944.550
Services	10.300.000	10.300.000	10.300.000	10.300.000	10.300.000	10.300.000	123.600.000
Energy	65.191.671	64.560.174	63.521.766	66.079.971	65.364.516	65.441.166	688.633.620
Other costs	2.575.000	2.575.000	2.575.000	2.575.000	2.575.000	2.575.000	30.900.000
Load costs	86.978.055	85.584.265	85.096.150	87.891.903	86.996.433	86.659.431	938.808.558
Transformation costs	125.638.444	123.910.911	122.785.473	127.118.528	125.860.393	125.572.251	1.348.241.979
Amortization	14.111.667	14.111.667	14.111.667	14.111.667	14.111.667	14.111.667	169.340.000
Transformation costs	139.750.111	138.022.578	136.897.140	141.230.195	139.972.059	139.683.917	1.517.581.979
Product costs	155.628.192	153.745.050	152.367.649	157.322.886	155.887.770	155.618.147	1.685.258.901

To calculate the cost price of our products, we must divide the costs into variable costs, relatively fixed, and fixed costs.

Mon. Unit	Year	Var	Fix	Var mon unit	Fix mon unit	Var mon unit /h	Fix mon unit /h
Production volume	2.893.419						
Direct hours	524.915						
Basic material							
Product A	151.421.080						
Product B	16.255.842						
Total	167.676.922	100%		167.676.922	-		
Direct work	409.433.421	100%		409.433.421	-	780	-
Indirect work	13.629.330	70%	30%	9.540.531	4.088.799	18	8
Administration	18.101.058		100%	-	18.101.058	-	34
Packaging material	63.944.550	85%	15%	54.352.868	9.591.683	104	18
Services	123.600.000		100%	-	123.600.000	-	235
Energy	688.633.620	50%	50%	344.316.810	344.316.810	656	656
Other costs	30.900.000		100%	-	30.900.000	-	59
Load costs	938.808.558			408.210.209	512.497.291	778	976
Transformation costs	1.348.241.979			817.643.629	512.497.291	1.558	976
Amortization	169.340.000		100%	-	169.340.000	-	323
Transformation costs	1.517.581.979			817.643.629	681.837.291		
Product costs	1.685.258.901			985.320.551	681.837.291		

Based on these data, we can calculate the amount of transformation costs per unit of the finished product. Transformation costs are those costs that we need to transform the material into a finished product and include production costs other than material costs. By adding the cost of materials per unit and the cost of transformation per unit, we get the cost price of our finished products in the budget, which in our case is 572 for product A and 613 for product B.

	Product A	Product B
Material	58	58
Variable costs	1.558	1.558
Fixed costs	1.299	1.299
Transformation costs	2.857	2.857
Hours of making	0,18	0,19
Transformation costs	514	556
Cost price	572	613

As with efficiency, prices can be compared and observed at all production costs. For this example, we assumed that cost prices remained the same throughout the year. This is generally not the case in practice, on the contrary, if the analysis of variances done during the year, as well as budget revisions done during the year, show the need to adjust cost prices. This must be done if the company wants to operate positively and maximize its profit in accordance with the plan and goals.

We will start the discussion with variance in the price of direct materials. Since the share of direct material in many industries is significant, deviation from the planned price can cause large changes and deviations in the overall cost of materials, and thus increase the cost price. That is why in most industries the prices of direct materials must be monitored with great care. The procurement sector and, of course, the procurement manager are responsible for monitoring and managing the prices of direct materials. In case of deviation from the plan, the reason and possible corrective measures must be known so that a potential solution can be sought afterward. In our example, this is not the case because the participation of the material is small.

In addition to direct materials, labor costs also represent a significant share of the cost price. As already mentioned, the Human Resources Department is responsible for the wage policy, however, the management of working hours is under the responsibility of the heads of individual sectors. What does that actually mean? Any additional or unplanned payment of salaries affects both the increase in the hourly rate of direct and indirect workers, as well as the salaries of employees in the administration. If overtime work is not planned or is higher than planned, additional work on weekends and holidays in relation to the plan also leads to an increase in labor costs, which is explained by the deviation or variance in the price of labor. Each manager is responsible for managing the working hours of their people and must ensure that labor costs are kept under control and within the planned values so that there are no deviations, otherwise each of them must explain what caused the deviation and find solutions to the situation.

In the processing industries, mostly construction, metal, and even automobile, energy costs are high, so negotiating future trends and contracting energy prices is crucial. We get the variance of the planned price when the difference between the planned and the current price is multiplied by the current consumed quantities.

In practice, the change in prices also happens on the side of income, i.e. sales. They can also very well influence a company's performance and they certainly need to be taken into consideration when analyzing the results. The Sales Director is of course responsible for price deviations and their explanation.

In this example, we have predicted positive price variations in production in the total amount of 53.3 million, of which: direct material of 11.5 million, packaging material of 1 million, and energy of 40.8 million. On the other hand, we have a negative impact on sales prices of 101.7 million.

Variances in price					
	Bdg	Vol Mix	Flex	Efficiency	Price
Production volume	2.893.419	122.895	3.016.314	0	0
Direct hours	524.915	22.296	547.210	0	0
Working days	232	0	232	0	0
Costs of direct material	167.677	7.122	174.799	-2.636	-11.486
Direct Labor Costs	409.433	17.390	426.824	-7.835	0
Indirect Work	13.629	405	14.035	608	0
Administration	18.101	0	18.101	43	0
Labor costs	441.164	17.796	458.959	-7.183	0
Packaging material	63.945	2.716	66.661	110	-980
Services	123.600	0	123.600	1.191	0
Energy Costs	688.634	14.625	703.258	-26.412	-40.820
Other Costs	30.900	0	30.900	9.056	0
Load Costs	938.809	17.746	956.554	-15.404	-41.800
Transformation Costs	1.348.242	35.136	1.383.378	-23.239	-41.800
Amortization	169.340	0	169.340	5.442	0
Total costs of Transformation	1.517.582	35.136	1.552.718	-17.797	-41.800
Total Production Costs	1.685.259	42.258	1.727.517	-20.433	-53.286
Change in inventory value					
The cost of the sale	1.685.259	42.258	1.727.517	-20.433	-53.286
Distribution costs	179.655		179.655	7.593	0
Administration costs	67.667		67.667	5.465	0
COGS	1.932.581	42.258	1.974.839	-7.375	-53.286
Total sales	2.653.282	118.488	2.771.770	0	101.736
Result	720.702	76.230	796.932	7.375	-48.450

The analysis of the variance of the results always compares two perspectives of the same periods. It is usually one year or period, and the previous year is compared, with the plan and realization of the current year. Thus, in our example, on the one hand, we have the planned result, which after realization we correct for the realized level of production or sales. On the other hand, there are the actual costs of production and the actual revenues from the sale of finished products. The differences that exist between these values for each cost and revenue line are explained using efficiency price variations. The variance of the exchange rate can be included in the analysis if the company is in some way connected with abroad in terms of ownership, purchase of materials, and sale of finished products abroad, but for the purposes of this example, we have remained within the domestic economy.

Analysis of variance, with actual achievement	Bdg	Vol Mix	Flex	Efficiency	Price	Achievement
Production volume	2.893.419	122.895	3.016.314	0	0	3.016.314
Direct hours	524.915	22.295	547.210	0	0	547.210
Working days	232	0	232	0	0	232
Direct material costs	167.677	7.122	174.799	-2.636	-11.486	160.677
Direct labor costs	409.433	17.390	426.824	-7.835	0	418.989
Indirect Work	13.629	406	14.035	608	0	14.643
Administration	18.101	0	18.101	43	0	18.144
Labor costs	441.164	17.796	458.959	-7.183	0	451.776
Packaging material	63.945	2.716	66.661	110	-980	65.790
Services	123.600	0	123.600	1.191	0	124.791
Energy Costs	688.634	14.625	703.258	-26.412	-40.820	636.026
Other Costs	30.900	0	30.900	9.056	0	39.956
Load Costs	938.809	17.746	956.554	-15.404	-41.800	899.350
Transformation Costs	1.348.242	35.136	1.383.378	-23.239	-41.800	1.318.339
Amortization	169.340	0	169.340	5.442	0	174.782
Total costs of Transformation	1.517.582	35.136	1.552.718	-17.797	-41.800	1.493.121
Total Production Costs	1.685.259	42.258	1.727.517	-20.433	-53.286	1.653.798
Change in inventory value						
The cost of the sale	1.685.259	42.258	1.727.517	-20.433	-53.286	1.653.798
Distribution costs	179.655		179.655	7.593	0	187.248
Administration costs	67.667		67.667	5.465	0	73.131
COGS	1.932.581	42.258	1.974.839	-7.375	-53.286	1.914.178
Total sales	2.653.282	118.488	2.771.770	0	101.736	2.670.034
Result	720.702	76.230	796.932	7.375	-48.450	755.857

In addition to the tabular overview, the graphical overview gives a better overview from which we can quickly notice deviations in responsibilities.

Price variations

The correction of the results of 76.2 million is explained by the difference in absorption and the mix of production and sales (volume mix).

When it comes to price variance, the variance of the selling price is especially singled out due to the great influence on the overall result. In this case, the company expressed 101.7 million is the negative effect of sales prices.

In terms of production costs, we have the largest reduction in energy prices as a result of the gas price correction. Then, better entry prices for direct materials and packaging of 12.5 million were achieved.

The company generated an efficiency of transformation costs of 17.8 million. Efficiency in direct material of 2.6 million, direct work 7.8 million, the company has achieved by managing to reduce production time per unit of product A by 5% by optimizing some operations, which further led to less involvement of direct labor. The company has shown inefficiency in the indirect work and costs of administrative staff. On the other hand, in the costs of services and other production costs, we have an inefficiency of 9.2 million. The company generates the highest efficiency in energy costs, which are also the largest generator of production costs.

The fixed costs of sales and administration (Overheads) are also slightly higher compared to the previous period. This is caused by the increased costs of fairs and additional employment of sales representatives in the markets to which entry is planned in the future.

Depreciation costs are also higher than planned, mostly due to the acceleration of new investments, which led to higher depreciation costs of newly activated assets.

In addition to these deviations, some deviations do not occur regularly but appear as unplanned only once. They are treated in this way and are shown in the analysis only in case of occurrence.

T-test method

A company is offering an investment opportunity that guarantees variable but attractive month to month returns. An investor that is looking to invest in new opportunities, is willing to take a risk on the off chance that he is guaranteed an average pay of 200 a month. There is a particular investment that has a history of 150 months' profits. It has a mean pay of 210 and a standard deviation of 85. Would it be a good idea for him to put resources into this plan? Let's use the t-test method to decide:

H_0: Null Hypothesis: mean = 200

H_1: Alternative Hypothesis: mean > 200

$$Z = \frac{\overline{X} - \mu}{\sigma/\sqrt{n}}$$

From this, the condition becomes:

$$Z \geq Z_{\alpha}$$

Z= (210 – 200) / (85 / sqrt (150)) = 2.882

The rejection region (from the z table) at a 5% significance level is Z> $Z_{0.05}$ = 1.645. So, this means that Z has to be greater than 1.645 for a greater than 95% chance of the investment yielding more than 200.

As in this case Z= 2.882, which is a higher value than the conditional value of 1.645, the null hypothesis can be rejected. There is a more than 95% possibility of the average monthly incentive to be greater than 200, and the investor should take the risk.

This can be shown on a graph:

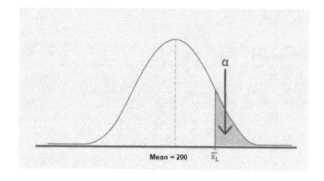

Decision Making Using Statistics

Economics is the science of meeting human needs, which provides knowledge of a qualitative nature. This does not mean, however, that mathematical methods and models have not been applied in economic research. Primarily because in almost all pores of economic life we find the need to measure, count, i.e. to quantitatively express numerical knowledge.

Mathematical - statistical methods are used to analyze the assumptions and consequences of a possible decision, while the decision itself is always only an economic problem, although, in reality, it is not logical to separate the economic from the mathematical problem.

The application of the given models, the realization of its characteristics provides the possibility that every business decision is based on the greatest possible efficiency and that every economic problem is optimized, which leads to the realization of economic principles.

We are going to take the case of the company in the ANOVA example, to see how statistics can help in the decision making process.

139

To obtain the selling price, we assume that it is 36% higher than the cost price, so the obtained sales prices are as in the table below. In practice, the sales department, based on market movements and competition, creates a pricing policy based on which revenues are calculated. Also, within the same process, the sales department submits its costs related to storage and distribution, general costs of sales, marketing. The same applies to the costs of administration, HR, IT, etc.

	Product A	Product B
Material		
	58	58
Variable costs	1.558	1.558
Fixed costs	1.299	1.299
Transformation costs	2.857	2.857
Hours of making	0,18	0,19
Transformation costs	514	556
Cost price	572	613
Profit margin 36%	341	341
Sales price	913	954

After calculating the sales price based on sales quantities, we receive revenue and can create a complete Income Statement. The budget prepared in this way is ready for approval by the Company's Management.

140

Mon unit	Jan	Feb	Mar	Apr	May	jun
Production volume	150.018	139.434	155.460	260.395	282.668	266.119
Direct hours	27.380	25.442	28.379	47.253	51.267	48.168
Basic material						
Product A	7.192.200	6.712.720	7.431.940	13.575.660	14.847.140	14.368.200
Product B	1.495.846	1.362.581	1.571.103	1.514.110	1.534.235	1.057.493
Total	8.688.046	8.075.301	9.003.043	15.089.770	16.381.375	15.425.693
direct Work	21.356.775	19.844.493	22.135.673	36.857.341	39.988.298	37.571.078
indirect work	1.100.385	1.061.775	1.293.435	1.177.605	1.177.605	1.293.435
Administration	1.511.248	1.512.500	1.507.500	1.509.750	1.509.750	1.507.500
Packaging material	3.315.401	3.081.483	3.435.675	5.754.740	6.246.952	5.881.225
Services	10.300.000	10.300.000	10.300.000	10.300.000	10.300.000	10.300.000
Energy	35.704.321	33.185.199	36.999.581	61.974.119	67.274.871	63.336.266
Other costs	2.575.000	2.575.000	2.575.000	2.575.000	2.575.000	2.575.000
Load costs	54.506.355	51.715.957	56.111.192	83.291.213	89.084.178	84.893.425
transformation costs	75.863.130	71.560.450	78.246.865	120.148.554	129.072.476	122.464.504
Amortization	14.111.667	14.111.667	14.111.667	14.111.667	14.111.667	14.111.667
Transformation Costs	89.974.797	85.672.116	92.358.531	134.260.221	143.184.143	136.576.170
Product costs	98.662.842	93.747.417	101.361.574	149.349.991	159.565.518	152.001.863
Distribution costs	14.971.250	14.971.250	14.971.250	14.971.250	14.971.250	14.971.250
Administration costs	5.638.904	5.638.904	5.638.904	5.638.904	5.638.904	5.638.904
Sale						
In total	138.033.178	128.274.466	143.055.634	238.820.678	259.169.427	243.720.469

Mon unit	Jul	Aug	Sept	Oct	Nov	Dec	Yearly
Production volume	273.915	271.261	266.898	277.647	274.641	274.963	2.893.419
Direct hours	49.565	49.137	48.320	50.291	49.826	49.888	524.915
Basic material							
Product A	14.847.140	14.494.340	14.368.200	14.847.140	14.368.200	14.368.200	151.421.080
Product B	1.030.941	1.228.132	1.102.309	1.245.551	1.547.511	1.566.029	16.255.842
Total	15.878.081	15.722.472	15.470.509	16.092.691	15.915.711	15.934.229	167.676.922
direct Work	38.660.389	38.326.646	37.689.323	39.226.625	38.863.960	38.912.820	409.433.421
indirect work	1.351.350	646.718	1.293.435	1.293.435	1.177.605	762.548	13.629.330
Administration	1.506.522	1.507.500	1.507.500	1.507.500	1.509.750	1.504.038	18.101.058
Packaging material	6.053.512	5.994.873	5.898.450	6.135.997	6.069.562	6.076.680	63.944.550
Services	10.300.000	10.300.000	10.300.000	10.300.000	10.300.000	10.300.000	123.600.000
Energy	65.191.671	64.560.174	63.521.766	66.079.971	65.364.516	65.441.166	688.633.620
Other costs	2.575.000	2.575.000	2.575.000	2.575.000	2.575.000	2.575.000	30.900.000
Load costs	86.978.055	85.584.265	85.096.150	87.891.903	86.996.433	86.659.431	938.808.558
transformation costs	125.638.444	123.910.911	122.785.473	127.118.528	125.860.393	125.572.251	1.348.241.979
Amortization	14.111.667	14.111.667	14.111.667	14.111.667	14.111.667	14.111.667	169.340.000
Transformation Costs	139.750.111	138.022.578	136.897.140	141.230.195	139.972.059	139.683.917	1.517.581.979
Product costs	155.628.192	153.745.050	152.367.649	157.322.886	155.887.770	155.618.147	1.685.258.901
Distribution costs	14.971.250	14.971.250	14.971.250	14.971.250	14.971.250	14.971.250	179.655.000
Administration costs	5.638.904	5.638.904	5.638.904	5.638.904	5.638.904	5.638.904	67.666.853
Sale							
In total	250.819.121	248.537.221	244.464.027	254.379.786	251.850.513	252.157.757	2.653.282.276
The result	74.580.775	74.182.017	71.486.224	76.446.746	75.352.588	75.929.456	720.701.523

CONCLUSION

This book is not intended to impose an obligation to entrepreneurs and companies to apply certain model or way of work, but an intention to indicate in which direction they want to go, i.e. what these methods include and in what ways measure business performance with special emphasis on key assumptions for measuring performance. Namely, for quality financial management, it is necessary to consider the success of the business, and the above basic prerequisites are key to measuring performance. Fulfilling these preconditions, i.e. developing both short and long term planning, setting measurable goals for which we have envisaged quality measures and establishing a link between them and budget funds, as well as the existence of well-defined indicators will help you measure performance, regardless of the method and steps you apply.

In this process of measuring performance, reports that link financial parameters with non-financial parameters are of special importance, because reporting provides feedback on performance, which can lead to changes in existing strategic plans or improve future strategic plans (better goals, better-prepared measures, better definition of indicators, a better connection of goals and budget funds, etc.).

In financial management, the institution is obliged to take into account the application of the principle of "value for money", which means that in providing services to clients, quality standards are met and that it is done economically and efficiently, i.e. to spend as little money as possible and provide quality service.

We are grateful for the time you have invested in reading this book. We truly hope that it will help you in the process of making efficient decisions that cover the area of capital structure, working capital, investment decisions, and maintaining liquidity.

In the end, in case you are interested in further readings, we recommend few books to start with.

- Financial Intelligence, Revised Edition: A Manager's Guide to Knowing What the Numbers Really Mean (by Karen Berman, Joe Knight, and John Case), Harvard Business Review Press, 2013

- Cost Accounting Made Simple: Cost Accounting Explained in 100 Pages or Less (by Mike Piper), Simple Subjects, LLC, 2017

- Accounting QuickStart Guide: The Simplified Beginner's Guide to Financial & Managerial Accounting For Students, Business Owners and Finance Professionals (by Josh Bauerle), ClydeBank Media LLC, 2016

- How Finance Works: The HBR Guide to Thinking Smart About the Numbers (by Mihir Desai), Harvard Business Review Press, 2019